THE DIPLOMATS

BY

MARTIN SCHWARTZ

The Diplomats
by Martin Schwartz
Dark Porch Theatre

Copyright © 2016
by Martin Schwartz
All rights reserved

Published by EXIT PRESS

Book design by Richard Livingston & C White

CAUTION: Professionals and amateurs are hereby warned that the play represented in this book is subject to a royalty. All rights of every kind to the play belong to the playwright, Martin Schwartz.

Please direct performance inquiries to
Martin Schwartz
3979A 17th Street
San Francisco, CA 94114
mhschwar@gmail.com

For additional information about
EXIT PRESS, go to
www.exitpress.org

ISBN: 978-1-941704-09-7

EXIT PRESS
156 Eddy Street
San Francisco, CA 94102-2708
mail@theexit.org

First Edition: May 2016

Author's Preface

While I have, as an adult, lived nowhere but San Francisco, I have seen and known the world of *The Diplomats*. By the time you read this, I will have spent fully one quarter of my life in the paid employ of a foreign state. You see, I work at a diplomatic representation. Though my business cards read a little differently, the conventional title for the function I exercise is "cultural attaché." People often ask how it came to be that a playwright from Marin practices cultural diplomacy for a European nation. I will tell you how.

Eight years ago, I responded to a job posting that seemed ready-made for me: the position called for critical thinking, cultural savvy, an advanced degree, connections in the Bay Area arts scene, and communications and foreign language skills on which I prided myself. The terms were generous. My application was well received, and soon enough the Deputy Consul General called me in for an initial interview. I remember my first time waiting in the lobby at the Consulate. I was awed and made small, struck especially by the bright, silvery lettering that ran up a pillar and designated this space as an official outpost of a foreign nation. Many times I saw my reflection in those letters during the weeks-long interview process. Many times I wondered what I, me, Martin Schwartz, could have to do with all this seriousness. And yet somehow the vetting came to its final iteration, and eventually I was granted an audience with the Consul General. Two men in suits ushered me into an improbably spacious corner office with blinding fenestration. They disappeared before I could turn around and say goodbye.

Bathed in light, the man himself sat before me. The Consul General took a very brief, very self-assured moment to review some papers before acknowledging me. He was a short man with close-cropped, receding hair. Shielded by his enormous desk and presided over by a large, limp flag, he wore square, bronze-rimmed spectacles and an exceedingly soft silk tie. His accent was thick and his voice soft as he half-rose and ceremoniously bade me sit on a comically low sofa. After the pleasantries, which thankfully got us started in English, he thoughtfully opened and examined my file. Crouching in silence on the sofa, nonplussed and outclassed, I had a moment of panic. What on earth was I doing here? But then I caught myself: that feeling—was it by chance stage fright? And then in that instant I sensed—I knew—that *this, all this*, was itself a type of theatre. And in the theatre—think quickly now—onstage, when you're in a scene, and something happens, what do you do? What drives you? Why, the given circumstances, of course. The ground rules. The world of the play, the world of your character. But who—quick!—who the hell was my character? I started observing and reacting to my setting, unconsciously calibrating my mood and physical expression. First of all, a certain posture, a certain tone. Sense of composure: softness and steadiness of voice. Sense of status—relative status—yes: inferior, but not a lackey. By no means a lackey. Hands? What to do with hands? One on your notebook, the other lightly curved, not clenched, on your knee. Feet on the floor, lower back locked in, shoulders inclined just slightly forwards. Good.

The Consul General looked up. He had, it seemed, decided to quiz me about "culture," but to do so in a way that is closely related to polite conversation. Improv. He mentioned a current show at the DeYoung Museum, a major retrospective of a pair of goofy British designer/artists. He'd happened to see it the previous weekend and asked me if I'd been. "And your impressions?" he asked, just barely a question. Visual art isn't my game, but I can rap. I said I had mixed feelings about it: I praised the graphical efficacy of the work, questioned its intentions, and commented gingerly on the subject matter (which was in actual fact fairly racy). He said he liked the show, but seemed to approve of my response. Note taken.

And then I won myself a job. There was an installation up at that time, at the more reputable of the local art schools, which was kicking up rather a stir. As I recall, it featured a video in which dogs, in some miserable factory in Mexico, were slaughtered with a hammer. Outcry: animal lovers. I believe the school, under public pressure, closed the show. The Consul General casually picked up a newspaper in front of him, then tossed it away. "This story," he asked, "about the art with the dogs. You have heard of it?" Why certainly (I'd fortunately read the paper myself that morning). "And what do you think?" I told him that I personally believe in the right and responsibility of art to be controversial; that I personally don't find anything objectionable about the material. After all, the artist wasn't killing the dogs. Pause. That said, I added, *my character added*, I could naturally—*naturally!*—understand that, from an *institutional* perspective, there might be certain reasons for caution, for reconsideration, or at least for public dialogue…

Two minutes later, as the Consul General concluded the audience, he thanked me. I thanked him. "I hope that we can take a decision soon," he said. I thanked him again, he thanked me again, and we shook hands. "But I cannot be sure when you will be informed," he added. "After all," he mused with a minute smile as the men in suits led me away, "I am not a secretary."

Thus began the process by which this play was conceived. And inevitably, the genre to which it aspires is Comedy.

Allow me to offer two footnotes to the play. First, about the *Mamamouchi*, that ceremony that completes young Larry's process of entente with the uncontrollable forces of theatricality: The term *Mamamouchi* is, to the best of my knowledge, gibberish, coined by

Molière in *The Bourgeois Gentleman*. In that venerable *comédie-ballet* about the hopeless mess that status envy can inflict on the keenest minds, the eponymous would-be nobleman, M. Jourdain, is duped into consenting to his daughter's marriage to a suitor posing as the son of the Grand Turk. The play ends with a long, surreal, and nonsensical ritual in which M. Jourdain is grandly and spuriously invested with a fantastical, imaginary title, one far nobler (he thinks) than those of all the courtiers he envies. That title is, of course, *Mamamouchi*. While in *The Diplomats*, *Mamamouchi* is used to describe both the ceremony and the title it confers, I venture to hope Molière would not have minded my appropriating his terminology.

And second, a word about historical events. In 2005, in the city of Andijan, Uzbekistan, security forces killed between somewhere between nine (according to the Uzbek government) and 1,500 (according to witnesses) civilian protesters. The proximal causes of the protests and the ensuing response are debated. Uzbekistan blamed Islamist fundamentalist terrorists for the demonstrations. NGOs pointed out the government's irregular imprisonment of 23 prominent businessmen. The US government response was swift and equivocal. Uzbekistan was a strategic ally: the US Military organized key operations through the air base in Karshi-Khanabad. According to the *Washington Post*, Secretary Rumsfeld opposed an international inquiry into the Andijan massacre at a NATO ministerial meeting, and one never took place. Islam Karimov, President of Uzbekistan since 1990, is still in power today. *The Diplomats* is set in an unnamed Central Asian "republic"—but while Central Asia is vast, the play's "completely justified security measures" cannot have been taken so very far from Andijan.

My profound thanks, for this edition and for the space and support to help mount *The Diplomats* and many other plays, to Christina Augello and Richard Livingston of The EXIT. To my dramaturg and friend Garret Jon Groenveld for years of insightful and creative readings. To my theatre partner, Margery Fairchild, without whose gifts I would be a much poorer stage artist. To my wife, Katherine Brumage, whose love afforded me the joy it took to write *The Diplomats*. And it would be ungracious of me indeed not to express my sincere gratitude to my employer, which has fed, clothed, and taught me for many years.

Martin Schwartz
San Francisco, March, 2016

The Diplomats

A Comedy

By Martin Schwartz

Dramatis Personae

(Actors Required: 7-20)

<u>Members of the Troupe "The Cultural Attachés"</u>

TWO: Male. 40s-50s.

THREE: Flirty Ingénue-type. 20s-30s.

FOUR: Leading Lady-type. 40s. Beautiful black hair.

FIVE: Old Pro-type. Silver-haired doyen.

SIX: Female, age open. The true-believer comedy Bolshevik of their little cell.

<u>The Diplomats</u>

J. LAWRENCE FISHBEIN: Around 30, Jewish. American cultural attaché. Going through a crisis of roles: his performance as the character of the diplomat has become both exhausting and inescapable. Trouble compartmentalizing. Panic attacks.

PIERRE-FRANÇOIS: French cultural attaché, 40s. Irritable, punctilious, obnoxiously soft-spoken, wears bronze-rimmed glasses and soft silk ties. Extremely heavy accent. Played by TWO.

RENATE: 20s-30s. German cultural attaché. Young, nubile, naïve but intellectually sophisticated. Classics degree. Genuine. Sexually voracious. Says what she means. Blouses and white Birkenstocks. Played by THREE.

CATHERINE: British cultural attaché, 40s. Exquisitely groomed, gay woman, wears black suits with skirts and blinding white shirts. Very feminine. Depressed, jaded, a veteran with no illusions. Played by FOUR.

THE AMERICAN AMBASSADOR: The very type of the American diplomat, white hair, formal but not courtly; direct-sounding speech that usually imports nothing. Played by FIVE.

AMERICAN EMBASSY SECRETARY: Texan charm. Disarming informality. Magical power beyond her station. Played by SIX.

DEPUTY MINISTER OF INFORMATION: Head of Department of Culture. Educated, fundamentally barbaric Central Asian technocrat. 30s-40s. Habituated to power on a medium to high level. Nephew of the "President."

ASSISTANT DEPUTY MINISTER: Old-fashioned functionary with thick specs, a Soviet-era cardigan, cheap tie, and moustache. Can be played by TWO.

Assorted Peons, Thugs, Torturers, Stagehands, Spearholders, Great Aunts, et al. double cast as circumstances dictate.

Time: 2005.

Setting: The scene is laid in the newly build capital city of a Central Asian "republic" in a politically tense period. Increasingly vociferous public protest incites increasingly violent repression. Interludes with the actors take place in the theatre: a stripped, black stage.

Note: In Act I, Scene V and again in Act III Scene I, the diplomats' dialogue in columns is spoken simultaneously until all are cued to stop.

Prologue

At rise: Bare stage. Brass-driven bullfight music plays, repeats, crescendos. Music out. Enter LARRY, in khaki slacks, a blue blazer, and conservative tie, holding a leather briefcase.

LARRY (*confidently puts out his hand*) J. Lawrence Fishbein, US Embassy—

Bullfight music hits, quite loud. LARRY jumps, freezes, hands and legs splayed. SIX enters, in a mask. Enter THREE, also in a mask.

SIX Do we do it or not?

THREE Hmm?

SIX Just a moment.

SIX hits LARRY with a huge powder pouf. Spotlight on LARRY. LARRY's legs, arms, hands shake and shiver, a snatch of the music, then out. Enter TWO, masked.

TWO The festival, dummy.

Enter FIVE, masked.

FIVE Why on earth not?

FOUR Yes: the show is grand. We're grand.

THREE But the government; the…thing

FIVE (*pantomiming shooting a machine gun while SIX pantomimes being shot*) The Completely Justified Security Measures Against Terrorist Agitation.

THREE Do we really want to play along?

FOUR Are we playing along if we just do our little show?

THREE We'll see how he likes our letter.

SIX Yes. Cloak of Jollity.

THREE Enough about the cloak!

FIVE Don't forget the scepter. (*Produces the scepter, smacks SIX with it.*)

SIX Ow! And the Scepter of Satire.

FOUR Fine. (*Sotto voce*) Should we, er—

SIX Ooh! Of course!

The music hits. A sparkly neon sign is lowered, flashing: "The West Laughs!" LARRY runs off, shrieking.

SIX (*cont.*) Ah, yes. The West laughs.

Act I Scene I

Music plays during transition. American Embassy. A large door on casters slants downstage right to upstage center, separates the meeting room from the foyer. A large green table set diagonally dominates the large, spare meeting room. American flag on a pole in a corner. Big poster for the festival, reading "The West Laughs! Comic Theatre Festival."

LARRY sticks his head out, walks out timidly, paces, mutters his name, pulls his hair in the dim foyer. Tries to steel himself to open the door to the meeting room, puts his hand on the handle, can't quite take it, slaps himself, runs back and forth.

Lights up on meeting room as CATHERINE enters into it from the opposite side. She's in a black suit, white shirt, and silk neckerchief, wearing very dark sunglasses and carrying a beautiful leather bag. Takes a few steps coldly into the room, sneers. Turns around to make sure there's no one there. Drops her bag on the table. Removes her makeup kit, puts it on the table. Sits, facing out. Looks around again. Removes sunglasses. Emits the beginning of a long, ugly, weepy crying jag. Turns around, hears someone. Very rapidly, as though she's practiced in this, dries her tears, puts on her shades, opens her compact, quickly removes her shades and expertly fixes her face. Puts shades back on, composes herself with one or two deep breaths.

Enter PIERRE-FRANÇOIS, or rather he lurches in, holding his belly. Also in dark suit and sunglasses, with a leather briefcase. Wheezing, one hand with a handkerchief over his mouth. Founders against the table, wipes his face with the hankie. CATHERINE watches him coolly. He vocalizes. Sees CATHERINE. Straightens himself out. Removes shades, straightens tie, stands stiffly, wipes his brow with a handkerchief, and makes a slight bow.

PIERRE-FRANÇOIS Good morning. (*Pause*)

CATHERINE Okay.

PIERRE-FRANÇOIS Mon Dieu it is hot outside.

CATHERINE organizes her papers and things.

PIERRE-FRANÇOIS (*cont.*) I have had a terrible night.

CATHERINE (*busily*) Right.

PIERRE-FRANÇOIS (*easing himself into a chair*) My indigestion.

CATHERINE Lovely.

PIERRE-FRANÇOIS It was atrocious.

> *CATHERINE cautiously removes her glasses and fleetingly checks her face in her compact.*

PIERRE-FRANÇOIS (*cont.*) Up and down and up and down. I tell you, zis climate…

> *CATHERINE delicately leans her forehead on her hands.*

PIERRE-FRANÇOIS And I am sinking about my transfer all ze time. If zey send me to Geneva as zey promise, finally I will have peace. I must have peace!

CATHERINE You must have piss, Pierre-François?

> *Lights down in meeting room, lights up on LARRY by the door in the foyer. LARRY fiddles with his briefcase, paces, mutters to himself, looking for courage.*

LARRY J. Lawrence Fishbein, US Embassy. (*Louder*) J. Lawrence Fishbein, US Embassy.

> *Sticks out hand. Frightens himself. Pauses. Goes back to muttering his name, hears RENATE off, repeating a phrase in the local language, LARRY runs off. Lights on meeting room.*

RENATE "Prezidenti eng donolikdir. Prezidenti eng donolikdir." "The President is most wise."

> *RENATE enters, in tight trousers, sandals, and a silk short-sleeve blouse, with large earphones on, holding a Discman. She too wears sunglasses.*

RENATE (*cont.*) Donnerwetter is it hot out there! Hello, people!

> *CATHERINE tries quickly to compose herself.*

RENATE (*removing headphones and shades*) These language tapes are great! Now I know all de ways to praise the President.

CATHERINE I tried to learn the language my first posting, too. You'll get over it.

RENATE Where's Larry?

CATHERINE & PIERRE-FRANÇOIS (*checking their watches, simultaneously*) Late.

> *Lights dim in the meeting room, lights up on foyer, where LARRY strides in again, muttering his name to himself. He reaches for the door handle. EMBASSY SECRETARY enters discreetly.*

LARRY J. Lawrence Fishbein, US Embassy.

EMBASSY SECRETARY Of course you are, hon.

LARRY (*Affrights*) Ah!—It's you.

EMBASSY SECRETARY (*Removes makeup kit, starts fixing some on his face*) Y'all look a fright, Lar. Hold still.

> *Lights down foyer, up meeting room. RENATE takes in CATHERINE and PIERRE-FRANÇOIS. They both try to work up a smile.*

RENATE Wow. You two look terrible.

PIERRE-FRANÇOIS Yes, it is my indigestion.

CATHERINE Pierre-François, enough!

RENATE But what is wrong with you, Catherine?

CATHERINE Nothing! Nothing is wrong with me!

RENATE It is your Edwina?

CATHERINE (*breaking down*) It's Edwiiiiinaaaaa. She…(*suddenly stops crying, opens her arms*). Comfort me, love.

> *RENATE goes to CATHERINE.*

CATHERINE (*cont.*) Pierre-François, close your ears and stand in the corner.

PIERRE-FRANÇOIS What do you sink I am, a secretary?

CATHERINE Do it.

PIERRE-FRANÇOIS Ze honor of France does not permit—

CATHERINE Do it!

PIERRE-FRANÇOIS Eh bien. But just zis once!

> *PIERRE-FRANÇOIS goes into the corner. RENATE strokes CATHERINE's hair. Lights on foyer.*

EMBASSY SECRETARY Y'all are jumpy today.

LARRY (*Jumps*) Jumpy?! I'm sorry, I'm just a little—

EMBASSY SECRETARY What's been up with you, Lar?

LARRY Nothing. The usual.

EMBASSY SECRETARY The usual, Lar? (*LARRY makes to speak*) Hold still.

> *Lights on meeting room.*

RENATE Did you fight?

CATHERINE I'm thrown over. Tossed out like a hunk of putrid meat.

RENATE That is terrible! I am so sorry.

CATHERINE She said I have a shit career, and—

RENATE That is awful!

CATHERINE I know. She said if I had any self-respect at all I'd have gotten myself a posting in London years ago.

RENATE To be near her?

CATHERINE No. To kiss arse and get ahead. She's an Assistant Minister of State—

PIERRE-FRANÇOIS I am sorry—

CATHERINE & RENATE Shut up!

PIERRE-FRANÇOIS —but you have never kissed ze ass at head office?

Lights down on meeting room, up on foyer.

EMBASSY SECRETARY Y'all are shakin' like a cornstalk in a haystorm!

LARRY What?

Lights down on foyer, up on meeting room.

PIERRE-FRANÇOIS But zat is foolish not to kiss ze ass at HQ. I did it twice.

RENATE You had two tours kissing de ass at Quai d'Orsay?

PIERRE-FRANÇOIS Mais oui!

CATHERINE (*interrupting*) Pierre-François,

PIERRE-FRANÇOIS Yes?

CATHERINE You're still a cultural attaché.

PIERRE-FRANÇOIS Yes.

CATHERINE Middle aged.

PIERRE-FRANÇOIS (*considers*)—Yes.

CATHERINE Here.

PIERRE-FRANÇOIS …Yes.

CATHERINE And for all this you've wasted eight years browning your lips at head office?

PIERRE-FRANÇOIS I see your point.

CATHERINE —Shht. Now back you go.

PIERRE-FRANÇOIS returns to his corner. CATHERINE and RENATE silently high-five. Lights on foyer.

EMBASSY SECRETARY Now Larry if y'all keep twitching like that your face is gonna look like a coyote on a full moon!

LARRY What?

EMBASSY SECRETARY Shht. Almost done.

Lights on meeting room.

RENATE But you want to go to London anyway?

CATHERINE I've got to see her—yes.

RENATE Ooh, listen, the festival is a big project. Maybe you can request an early transfer right after.

CATHERINE You're a genius! Embrace me.

RENATE does so, somewhat warily. Lights on foyer.

EMBASSY SECRETARY I worry about you, Lar. Y'all got an important job to do.

LARRY It just gets to me—this festival—and what the hell are we doing about Mandijan?

EMBASSY SECRETARY What do you expect? Come on, Lar. (*LARRY about to speak*) Aaaand (*finishing touch*) done.

LARRY Thanks, doll.

EMBASSY SECRETARY Now, Mandijan or no Mandijan, y'all get in there and show those foreigners who's boss, y'hear? (*Slaps his rear*) God bless America!

> *EMBASSY SECRETARY opens the door, pushes LARRY into the doorway, disappears. LARRY freezes in doorway. All are interrupted by an air-raid siren, freeze in grotesque poses. Lights go down. A stern VOICE comes through loudspeakers in a Turkic language, overlapping with the same message repeated in tired, goofily read English.*

VOICE (*off*) Attention. Attention. Due to the events in Mandijan, special security measures will soon be in effect. Terrorist agitation severely punished.

Act I Scene II

All unfreeze. Lights up on meeting room. LARRY, in doorway, looks around. The others stare at him. He sticks out his hand.

LARRY J. Lawrence Fishbein, US Embassy.

PIERRE-FRANÇOIS We know zis.

CATHERINE looks at him peevishly.

CATHERINE You're late.

LARRY (*Sits, gets a file out of his briefcase*) Sorry, traffic.

RENATE Don't you live upstairs?

PIERRE-FRANÇOIS Zis is ridiculous, waiting. I am not a secretary.

RENATE You are not excited for the festival?

LARRY (*sits, opens his briefcase*) Well, I'm optimistic about the foreign policy relevance—

CATHERINE Of the festival? Please. They're bayoneting children on the courtyard square in Mandijan.

RENATE The crowds are bigger every day: it is a bad beginning.

CATHERINE Bayoneted children on the World Service <u>would</u> rather constitute a bad beginning.

LARRY Well, the international media has a certain bias against the president here—

CATHERINE Those silly children simply should have known protesting was a capital offense.

LARRY But he's been a real friend on international security.

PIERRE-FRANÇOIS It is a disgrace.

LARRY And the airbase is indispensable to NATO operations. You all have a different opinion on that ?

PIERRE-FRANÇOIS What about ze pipieline?

LARRY Oh yeah, the pipeline too.

RENATE But the brutality, Larry! What will the Americans do?

CATHERINE The Americans? The beacon of democracy?

LARRY We're looking into it.

PIERRE-FRANÇOIS Ze support of ze oppressed?

LARRY We've got an eye on the human rights situation—

CATHERINE (*overlapping*) The city on the hill?

PIERRE-FRANÇOIS Ze good guys?

LARRY I'm telling you we'll respond appropriately.

PIERRE-FRANÇOIS It is always the same.

LARRY Hey, that's not fair. There are complex geopolitical considerations; given the operations in the Gulf, this is a—

CATHERINE We know.

CATHERINE, RENATE, PIERRE-FRANÇOIS Nation of strategic importance.

LARRY Whoa—just a minute! Do our allies in NATO disagree with that statement? Well? Now listen to me, colleagues. No one cares about human rights more than the United States of America. (*Puts his hand on his heart.*)

RENATE Dat was very au-tho-ra-ta-tive, Larry!

LARRY The Ambassador is in daily contact with the local leadership about Mandijan—

PIERRE-FRANÇOIS Mais justement!

EMBASSY SECRETARY (*appearing from nowhere*) Hey, y'all go easy on Larry.

LARRY I can take care of myself—

EMBASSY SECRETARY He's real delicate right now. He's a little—

LARRY Hey!

EMBASSY SECRETARY (*Makes a "cuckoo" gesture, whispers*) Panic attacks.

LARRY (*blushing deeply*) That's not true! I—(*Takes out the file and begins reading it.*)

CATHERINE I thought he was a little at sea.

RENATE But he is so cute when he shows de backbone.

EMBASSY SECRETARY Ain't he just? (*EMBASSY SECRETARY disappears.*)

CATHERINE A diplomat must either be cunning and seem sincere or seem cunning and be sincere. Lots of Americans can't seem properly, and so they go bonkers.

PIERRE-FRANÇOIS Well said.

LARRY Once and for all I am a US Foreign Service officer on US Embassy property and I will not tolerate any denigration of the United States of America! (*hand on heart*) Do you hear me?

All hang their heads and murmur apologies.

RENATE So cute! (*Sizes him up, sidles towards him*) Aren't you, Larry.

LARRY (*blushing deeply*) Ah—thank you?…Now as the host of this meeting, can I formally request we get to work? The Deputy Minister is on his way and we have to confirm the schedule for the weekend.

CATHERINE Comic theatre with a massacre raging. The irony is too much.

RENATE Ja, I do not think that is irony sensu stricto, Catherine.

LARRY We have to see all sides of the situation, even if it looks like in flagrant delictee. (*As always, emphasizing and mispronouncing his bad Latin*) Now can we—

PIERRE-FRANÇOIS Zee authorities do not like the term "massacre." I believe zey call it ze "completely justified security measures against terrorist agitation."

LARRY Yes, exactly. The completely justified security measures against terrorist agitation.

CATHERINE Oh, yes. The (*every word in ironic quotes*) completely justified security measures against terrorist agitation.

RENATE The festival is good work, Catherine—maybe the festival will help the people.

LARRY Precisely. Intercultural exchange can—

CATHERINE (*overlapping*) Hmm. The Cultural Attachés are going to help the bayoneted children?

PIERRE-FRANÇOIS Only two bayoneted children so far.

RENATE Of course we will help.

LARRY Thank you, Renate.

CATHERINE Larry, shut up.

LARRY Excuse me!

CATHERINE Renate, you kill me, darling. The Culural Attachés. The theatre troupe…that's putting on The West Laughs!

PIERRE-FRANÇOIS Zewestloff?

RENATE Vat is vestloff?

LARRY Doing what?

CATHERINE The West Laughs! The West Laughs! Comic Theatre Festival.

PIERRE-FRANÇOIS But of course; do not talk at me like a child.

> *LARRY sighs deeply, starts going through the file in an obsessive way.*

LARRY I'm getting to work. I don't want to look like an idiot when the Deputy Minister gets here.

PIERRE-FRANÇOIS Bonne chance with zat.

CATHERINE My darling Renate, you actually believe the nonsense in the press release about laughter transcending misery? That's charming.

PIERRE-FRANÇOIS Excuse me, but for ze French Republic universal values are a matter of conviction…

RENATE Vell—

CATHERINE But what if they don't laugh? It's all in English, isn't it? (*Pause*) Do you even know where these clowns are from?

LARRY They're based in the U.S. But I think they're international. I can't quite tell—

RENATE Ja thanks Larry (*winks*). Listen, Catherine, they are very traditional comedians, the players, very physical. There is falling and hitting with schticks. De people have to laugh at dat!

CATHERINE Bet you dinner they don't.

PIERRE-FRANÇOIS Yes, excuse me, zis is the model on which we are working. Western comedy is universal and laughter supports mutual understanding; zis is why we have ze funding from ze NATO.

RENATE Ja, I studied classics and I sink dat no cultural expressions are really universal but Yes! We will laugh and the people will laugh with us. They laugh with the West, and stop fighting, and we laugh with them, and—

CATHERINE Why darling, you never told me you read classics! (*Clears throat*) "Quem Fors dierum cumque dabit, lucro"

> *RENATE girlishly excited.*

RENATE & CATHERINE "Adpone, nec dulcis amores / sperne puer neque tu choreas"[1]

---

1 "Leave off asking what tomorrow will bring, and / whatever days fortune will give, count them / as profit, and while you're young don't scorn / sweet love affairs and dances" – Horace, Odes, 1.9

RENATE (*cont.*) Dat is so great you know Latin.

CATHERINE We will have to discuss Horace over a very large bottle of Falernum.

> *CATHERINE winks. They giggle. LARRY looks up from file, locks eyes with RENATE, joins the giggling.*

LARRY Don't make me get a writ of habeas corpus against you two!

> *All stare at LARRY, who blushes.*
>
> *Enter EMBASSY SECRETARY carrying a bowl with fruits.*

EMBASSY SECRETARY Hey, y'all! The Deputy Minister is just at the security gate. And I thought y'all might want some fruit.

> *EMBASSY SECRETARY winks, sets the bowl down in front of PIERRE-FRANÇOIS, who glares at it in horror. EMBASSY SECRETARY exits.*

LARRY (*organizing his papers*) Oh, boy—quickly: as to the scheduling, on Friday there's the—

PIERRE-FRANÇOIS Larry, I have had a very bad night. Would you please remove zat bool?

CATHERINE Not this again.

> *CATHERINE leans over to RENATE, whispers in her ear. RENATE chuckles. CATHERINE leans in nearer, starts touching RENATE's hair while whispering during the following.*

LARRY What's a bool? Now, Thursday afternoon, that's today, arrival Cultural Attachés.

PIERRE-FRANÇOIS On ze table. The bool with ze—sings in it.

LARRY Does anyone see a bool with sings? So: Arrival, transfer to hotel in Embassy cars.

PIERRE-FRANÇOIS I have terrible stomach pains whenever I look at—certain sings.

LARRY Okay. Now, Thursday evening, walk through theatre venue, the "Great Gathering Place" of the whatever, light technical run thru—

PIERRE-FRANÇOIS Excuse me, this is urgent. This is PAIN. Not distaste. PAIN.

RENATE (*blushing, pushes CATHERINE away*) I am sorry.

LARRY Then bed. Friday morning: media conference, joined by Deputy Minister.

> *PIERRE-FRANÇOIS tries to cover the bowl with his jacket, then looks at the covered fruit and almost pukes.*

RENATE What is de problem, Pierre-François?

LARRY Heavy hors d'oeuvres. Full day rehearsal.

CATHERINE Bit of humor here. It's the fruit, is it?

PIERRE-FRANÇOIS (*overlapping*) (*Wincing at the word "fruit"*) Pain.

> *PIERRE-FRANÇOIS conquers his nausea and, guarding his mouth with his elbow, heaves himself towards the fruit basket and, holding it in front of him with two hands, tries to get rid of it, lurching about and nearly retching at every turn.*

LARRY Pierre-François, I'm sorry you're uncomfortable but can we at least review the schedule internally—

PIERRE-FRANÇOIS It is raw things, things that are not cooked.

LARRY (*overlapping*) —before the Deputy Minister—

> *PIERRE-FRANÇOIS then tries to put the basket it in a cabinet, it won't fit, bangs it against the door and sets off the alarm.*

LARRY (*over alarm, cont.*) Please—Pierre-François?—Friday, rehearsal, 7 p.m. photo ops—

PIERRE-FRANÇOIS (*interrupting*) My stomach is tremendously strong.

LARRY (*overlapping*) —red carpet. 8 p.m. curtain.

PIERRE-FRANÇOIS It is not weak, you must not insult it.

LARRY I wasn't insulting your stomach! I was just—

PIERRE-FRANÇOIS (*interrupting*) It is very, very strong for butter and meats and cream and things, you know, also custardy desserts.

CATHERINE Custardy desserts, eh?

LARRY (*still shouting over alarm*) Is this our top action item? (*Beat.*) Final curtain, 10 p.m. reception.

PIERRE-FRANÇOIS (*back to his stomach*) It is raw things from the earth. Around any raw foods, all of my insides search for the nearest sphincter and attempt to escape through it.

CATHERINE (*slightly amused*) I see.

LARRY Nearest sphincter? We need to get this together, people! (*Into intercom*) Can we turn off this alarm?

> *PIERRE-FRANÇOIS is staggering around the room howling; when he's in front of the door, it's opened and EMBASSY SECRETARY glares at him, takes the fruit, turns off the alarm, closes the door. Quiet.*

LARRY Can we get back on track?

PIERRE-FRANÇOIS (*Sweating, wiping his mouth with a silk handkerchief*) Excuse me, I was not being vulgar. Anatomy is not vulgar.

RENATE Ze body has many sphincters. So much fun to say! Sphincter.

PIERRE-FRANÇOIS This is prudish to sink zat anatomy is vulgar.

CATHERINE (*to PIERRE-FRANÇOIS*) Oh, shut up, you bloated letch.

RENATE I think the iris of the eye is also a sphincter.

> *LARRY continues to get his papers in order, one by one. He starts reading one with interest.*

LARRY Right. Might we—

RENATE Do your insides try to escape through your eye?

PIERRE-FRANÇOIS Yes, my friend. Zey do. Zey escape through tears.

LARRY (*tears at his hair*) We need to get this together, people!

CATHERINE Calm down, Larry! We mustn't look a fool in front of that fascist barbarian. (*LARRY is steaming*) Let's coordinate, or else all our next postings will be even worse than this one.

PIERRE-FRANÇOIS It's not so bad here. There are no flesh-eating parasites.

CATHERINE Now: The official reception is the only important part of the whole exercise. Do we have the wine?

PIERRE-FRANÇOIS (*Wiping his brow*) Yes.

CATHERINE Do we have the money?

LARRY Yes.

CATHERINE Do we have the little cocktail weenies?

RENATE Yes.

CATHERINE Funny, I thought that was Larry's department.

> *RENATE and CATHERINE snigger.*

LARRY (*finding something in the file that troubles him*) Colleagues—colleagues—colleagues—

CATHERINE Oh, shush, Larry.

RENATE Vat is it, my Yankee strudel?

LARRY Colleagues—

PIERRE-FRANÇOIS What is it?

LARRY Did you—did you read the last mail from the Cultural Attachés? The actors? From the—seventh?

>*All open their portfolios and snap to the correct page with a flourish.*

CATHERINE No.

PIERRE-FRANÇOIS I saw it.

RENATE I don't think so. Their letters are so funny though.

LARRY G—gg—gg-gggggg—ggggg---gg-gg-gggggggggggg—

>*(SIX/EMBASSY SECRETARY enters, hits LARRY's face with a huge powder pouf, leaving him quite white, and leaves. LARRY shakes with fear.*

RENATE Gesundheit?

LARRY Ggg—gg—gg-g-g-g-g-g-g-gggggggggggggg (*begins to stand up as though choking and starts slapping the table*) gg gg gg gggggggggg-g-g-gggggggggggggg—grr-r-grr-rr—grr—grrrrrrrr-----gggg-rrr—r

>*The diplomats are concerned.*

ALL Larry! Larry! Are you alright?

>*All crowd around him. CATHERINE attempts the Heimlich and PIERRE-FRANÇOIS tries to scare him as though he has the hiccups. LARRY stands, thrusts out his hand, yells:*

LARRY J. Lawrence Fishbein, US Embassy. (*Suddenly, LARRY quiets down and sits down, with complete composure.*) Sorry. Just another Jewish neurotic here.

PIERRE-FRANÇOIS (*as though all is explained*) Ahh, bien sûr, il est juif.

RENATE Ach ja, Jewish? I knew it! Dat means dey circumcise you, right? What a primitive ritual! (*Looks hard at his crotch*) Dat is so erotic!

CATHERINE Renate!

RENATE Oops, sorry; I meant to say, "De German people have a solemn responsibility…"

CATHERINE (*to LARRY*) Now what the hell was that about.

LARRY Well…

RENATE Vell, I have never—mit a Jew—de historical trauma…

CATHERINE He's not the bloody Prophet Moses, love. He's just a regular Yank.

> *LARRY looks down at the paper, then throws his head back and begins making "ggggg" sounds again. CATHERINE slaps him. Head still back, sitting straight upright, he pushes the letter forward.*

LARRY Read it yourself.

PIERRE-FRANÇOIS Excuse me, read it myself? I'm not a secretary!

CATHERINE Give me that. (*Takes file.*) "We, the Cultural Attachés, are conscious of comedy's function in society, and its effects on power…" blah, blah, blah, "We make no mistake. Entertainment serves the state. The comic spirit, the ludic spirit we represent serves no one, no institution, no human….blah blah…brothers! and sisters!, blah blah. In the ludic spirit is the promise of our shared life…opposed to the complex of rank torture that feeds us or deprives us……renders impossible decisions—whom to betray? And how?—possible to make. The ludic spirit is a power you wield and wear, it a cloak, a magical cloak and a scepter: the scepter of satire and the cloak of jollity…

RENATE Is this comical?

LARRY Keep reading.

PIERRE-FRANÇOIS Sceptre of satire?

RENATE Cloak of jollity?

LARRY Keep reading.

CATHERINE Ah, here it is. "We have decided, in light of the government repression at Mandijan, that the instrumentalization of our comedy by state power, especially by a state so blood-guilty as the one to which we have been invited, is grotesque in a not-funny way, and may outweigh the pure good of laughter itself. We will come to your so-called republic, but if we do not hear that your governments have taken a clear and principled stand against this brutal tyranny, we will refuse to be seen with you outside the theatre. No press conferences, no reception.

PIERRE-FRANÇOIS Mon Dieu, no reception?

LARRY You see what I mean?

CATHERINE Quiet, Larry! Did anyone write back to them? Well?

PIERRE-FRANÇOIS No, but…but zis is no way to communicate with the Embassy of France!

RENATE Scepter of satire?

LARRY G-gg-g-ggg-ggg--gg

CATHERINE Fucking hell. Liberia, here we come!

Act I Scene III

American Embassy. Same.

Enter EMBASSY SECRETARY.

EMBASSY SECRETARY Hey, Lar, the Deputy Minister is here.

LARRY This is the sinny quay non.

CATHERINE Enough bad Latin!

CATHERINE slaps LARRY. Turns her face away as though she had been the one to be slapped. PIERRE-FRANÇOIS nods at LARRY in sympathy.

RENATE Oh, man. Larry, you do not speak Latin.

With sadness, RENATE also slaps LARRY.

CATHERINE I'll never get to London now. (*To RENATE, opening her arms.*) Comfort me, love.

RENATE Jaaaa…(*looking at LARRY's crotch*) Now Larry, about your dingdong—

EMBASSY SECRETARY Uh, the Deputy Minister of Information is here for his appointment?!

LARRY (*with distraught irony*) Please show him in. Thank you.

Enter DEPUTY MINISTER. All rise. A clamor, "Your Excellency, Your Excellency," LARRY, as host, walks over to greet him. Exit EMBASSY SECRETARY. Others hang back nervously.

LARRY J. Lawrence Fishbein, US Embassy.

PIERRE-FRANÇOIS (*wheedling in, wiping the corner of his mouth with his handkerchief*) It is a pleasure to see you again, Your Excellency.

DEPUTY MINISTER The pleasure is mine, honorable consuls. And a very guten Tag to you, Fräulein. (*kisses RENATE's hand*)

RENATE Hi? Em, Excellency…

DEPUTY MINISTER (*cont.*) Please, there is no need for formality: "Your Excellency" is my father.

All chuckle.

DEPUTY MINISTER (*cont.*) No, really: he is my father.

CATHERINE Then how may we address you?

DEPUTY MINISTER You may call me Your Serene Munificence.

PIERRE-FRANÇOIS (*Beat*) Of course, Your Serene Magnificence.

DEPUTY MINISTER Munificence.

PIERRE-FRANÇOIS Munificence. Forgive me, Munificence.

LARRY Would Your Serene Munificence care to be seated?

DEPUTY MINISTER Thank you. (*Sits in LARRY's chair. A short bit. LARRY walks across the room to sit in the chair intended for DEPUTY MINISTER.*) The Ministry of Information is pleased for this opportunity to share in official cultural collaboration—

Nearly simultaneously.

PIERRE-FRANÇOIS As is ze Embassy of Fraunce.

CATHERINE As is the British Embassy.

RENATE As is the German Embassy.

LARRY As is the Embassy of the United States of America.

DEPUTY MINISTER —During your governments' unfortunate misunderstanding of our internal affairs. Our President himself mentioned the comic performance festival at a news conference this morning.

CATHERINE It's an honor to collaborate with the local authorities, sir.

DEPUTY MINISTER Your Serene Munificence.

CATHERINE Your Serene Munificence.

DEPUTY MINISTER Remind me of the name once more; was it "The Laughing NATO Countries Festival?"

RENATE The West Laughs! Comic Theatre Festival, Your Serene Munificence.

DEPUTY MINISTER Ah, yes, so clear. And the actors, they are called—

LARRY The Cultural Attachés, Your Serene Munificence.

DEPUTY MINISTER Ah yes, of course. It is funny: they are cultural attachés, you are cultural attachés.

All laugh warily.

DEPUTY MINISTER (*cont.*) You see, I have been rather preoccupied with the other performance festival, the one organized by your Russian, Iranian, and Chinese counterparts.

CATHERINE I've heard wonderful things about that, was it called the Friends Festival or something of that nature?

DEPUTY MINISTER It is named the "Remember Who Your Real Friends Are! Performing Arts Festival."

RENATE Great title!

DEPUTY MINISTER We just worked out the tagline. It is: "Russian Bears, Shiite Prayers, and Chinese Acrobats."

> *EMBASSY SECRETARY pokes in.*

EMBASSY SECRETARY (*to DEPUTY MINISTER*) Hey you, you want a coffee, hon?

> *All freeze, expecting that he is preparing to have a conniption about his title.*

DEPUTY MINISTER What? (*Beat*) Excuse me?

EMBASSY SECRETARY I was just asking the Deputy Minister if you wanted a coffee? Hon?

DEPUTY MINISTER (*Pause*) Oh, sorry. I couldn't hear you. No, thanks, doll—I've already had eight coffees this morning with lots of sugar. My kitchen staff is really insane—you have no idea! My teeth are chattering. I'm wired! Thanks for asking, though!

EMBASSY SECRETARY You'll take a rain check though, huh?

DEPUTY MINISTER Oh, for sure. I'll definitely take a rain check! I love American coffee!

EMBASSY SECRETARY Kay, hon.

DEPUTY MINISTER Bye-bye!

> *EMBASSY SECRETARY exits.*

DEPUTY MINISTER (*Immediately all seriousness*) My time is limited.

LARRY Shall we discuss the schedule, Your Serene Munificence?

DEPUTY MINISTER What is there to discuss? First there is the press conference, then there is the reception.

LARRY Don't forget about the performance, Munificence!

DEPUTY MINISTER Whatever. My government has made all of the necessary preparations. The venue, Great Gathering Place of the People, is scheduled and ready. The staff has been engaged. You have seen the lovely posters and very large announcements throughout the city.

ALL (*unison*) Of course, Munificence. They're beautiful, Munificence.

DEPUTY MINISTER We are proud of international cultural initiatives. Now all that is necessary is for the Cultural Attachés to arrive and perform. But not you! The other cultural attachés!

ALL (*unison*) Yes, yes, very funny, Serene Munificence.

DEPUTY MINISTER (*to LARRY*) Your Ambassador and the Minister will make introductions. About the order of introductions. We do not wish to insult the Ambassador.

LARRY And we do not wish to insult the Minister.

DEPUTY MINISTER Then who is first?

LARRY	**DEPUTY MINISTER**
The Ambassador?	The Minister.
LARRY	**DEPUTY MINISTER**
The Minister.	The Ambassador?

DEPUTY MINISTER Okay.

They play rock-paper-scissors. LARRY wins.

DEPUTY MINISTER Wait, I meant to do rock.

LARRY Best of three?

They do two more throws. The results are inconclusive. DEPUTY MINISTER takes out a coin. They both drop to one knee for the toss.

DEPUTY MINISTER Call in the air.

DEPUTY MINISTER tosses.

LARRY Heads! Heads! (*It's heads.*)

DEPUTY MINISTER Very well.

LARRY Best of three?

DEPUTY MINISTER No, it's all right. Actually both sides are heads on our coins.

LARRY How about they go up together.

DEPUTY MINISTER Deal.

They shake on it.

DEPUTY MINISTER (*cont.*) I assure you there will be a sizeable audience.

PIERRE-FRANÇOIS Your acumen is unprecedented.

DEPUTY MINISTER I believe the actors are expected at their hotel tonight for debriefing. I trust you will manage their transportation. To the reception.

LARRY (*Wants to go for the letter*) Of course—about that, Munificence…

DEPUTY MINISTER Just Munificence?

LARRY Serene Munificence, your Serene Munificence.

PIERRE-FRANÇOIS The wine has been delivered through ze diplomatic pouch.

RENATE And the little weenies.

DEPUTY MINISTER Good. Is there any delicious British food?

CATHERINE Delicious British food, Munificence? It's a reception, not a magic show.

> *CATHERINE starts going through the file, finds something extremely disturbing in it. She blanches.*

LARRY Serene Munificence, there may be a…

> *LARRY goes towards the file. CATHERINE frantically nods no, clutches it to her chest with a look of horror.*

DEPUTY MINISTER Thank you for your time. I must leave. That is all.

> *DEPUTY MINISTER exits. All rise, bow, except CATHERINE. Enter EMBASSY SECRETARY. To PIERRE-FRANÇOIS, in fluent, Texan French.*

EMBASSY SECRETARY Pardonnez-moi, monsieur?

PIERRE-FRANÇOIS Oui, madame?

EMBASSY SECRETARY On vous demande au téléphone.

PIERRE-FRANÇOIS A moi ?

EMBASSY SECRETARY C'est Paris, monsieur. Quay d'Orsay, y'all !

PIERRE-FRANÇOIS (*jumps up*) It is Paris! My promotion!

EMBASSY SECRETARY (*leads him out*) Par ici, monsieur.

RENATE Your secretary's good, Larry.

LARRY I had no idea she spoke French.

PIERRE-FRANÇOIS (*off, yells*) Mais non…mais NON! C'EST PAS POSSIBLE ÇA!

CATHERINE We have a problem.

PIERRE-FRANÇOIS (*entering alone, dejected*) Zis is..non, non.

RENATE What is it?

PIERRE-FRANÇOIS Ze head office—zey are worried about ze festival.

CATHERINE So am I.

PIERRE-FRANÇOIS I do not get my transfer to ze UN in Geneve unless ze festival goes perfectly. AND unless zere is not a single word about it in ze international press.

LARRY What? That doesn't make any sense!

CATHERINE Of course it does. They want to flatter the local government because of the pipeline and your damned air force base, but—

RENATE Ahhh, Mandijan. Dat is so cynical!

CATHERINE It's diplomatic. They don't want to catch any heat at home because of the—

PIERRE-FRANÇOIS Completely justified blah-blah-blah. Precisely.

LARRY That is an impossible situation, Pierre-François.

PIERRE-FRANÇOIS And it would be such a big promotion! I would be the assistant deputy deputy assistant junior deputy assistant assistant to ze assistant deputy deputy observer. Deputy.

LARRY I see.

PIERRE-FRANÇOIS Assistant. But (*retches, covers his mouth*) zere is worse. My position, ze assistant—

RENATE We got it.

PIERRE-FRANÇOIS Zey want to give it to my grand nemesis.

LARRY Your what?

> *CATHERINE's eyes are glued to the file in horror. Her jaw drops.*

PIERRE-FRANÇOIS My arch-enemy in ze department. He is insufferable! We were in ze same training volley in Paris. He is touchy and irritable; drunk and arrogant; he has a really obnoxious soft voice, and stupid self-indulgent health problems. And ze worst is he is always complaining about his career!

LARRY & RENATE (*Looking at each other quizzically*) I see…

CATHERINE (*quietly*) Ah—we have a problem.

RENATE What is his name?

PIERRE-FRANÇOIS François-Pierre.

LARRY Go figure.

CATHERINE No, really. We have a problem.

PIERRE-FRANÇOIS Anozer problem? Mais c'est pas possible, ça!

LARRY O tempura! O smores!

RENATE Stop it! You do not speak Latin, Larry! But seriously—

CATHERINE No, seriously. We have a problem.

LARRY (*his pride touched*) I'm no classics scholar, it is true, but I know a bit.

RENATE O tempora o mores means o the times o the customs.

LARRY That's what I meant. O what times!

RENATE No, Larry, customs, like your ritualistic penis-cutting, Larry: now does it hurt when you…

CATHERINE (*Nearly crying despite herself. Suddenly shouts*) Stop it! Shut up and listen.

PIERRE-FRANÇOIS Excuse me, I am not a—

A look from CATHERINE stops him cold.

CATHERINE "Not having heard from you or your governments"…blah blah… "Our performance would only inspire domestic and international support for this ignoble and unhappy regime, and so we must not perform. We are not coming to your so-called republic. We know the arrangements have been made, and the posters are everywhere. (*All look at the posters. Collective groan.*) "We intend this to embarrass you terribly: you and the foul dictatorship with which you have colluded."

PIERRE-FRANÇOIS But zis is outrageous!

A general wailing starts up: all begin to cry despite themselves.

CATHERINE (*weepy*) Edwinaaaa.

PIERRE-FRANÇOIS (*to CATHERINE*) Cherie, control yourself, all is not—

CATHERINE Shut up! I hate you, you perforated sack of sulfurous bile!

LARRY Listen—we need to—(*Hauls back and literally slaps himself out of it.*) Aaah. I'll go straight in to the Ambassador and talk it over. He said his door was always open.

Pause.

PIERRE-FRANÇOIS Well, go!

PIERRE-FRANÇOIS & RENATE & CATHERINE GO!

They push LARRY out the door.

Blackout.

Interlude 1

Bare stage. Dim. TWO, THREE, FOUR, FIVE, SIX, all masked. SIX is polishing the Scepter of Satire, a peculiarly phallic instrument that's also a working microphone. FIVE is dusting off the disco-shiny cloak of jollity. LARRY walks out, is hit by the spot.

SIX Comrades, comic-ists, do you feel this madness, this Babel? We will triumph.

FIVE Over what again?

SIX Over that. This diplomat, he forgets his context. We, in contrast, take roles upon ourselves and never once confuse them for the real thing.

THREE Now what was the real thing again?

TWO Get out of here, kid, you bother me.

THREE Where am I gonna go? Back into his head?

"Wind" blows. LARRY begins to shake.

TWO Is it time for the coffee break yet?

SIX This is the coffee break, moron.

THREE But what are we triumphing over again?

SIX We take aim at ceremony, at fooling that fools itself, at serious foolery. We have before us a man who cannot distinguish his life from his act. The one that is called: Larry.

LARRY Um, I can hear you?

THREE He's only trying to doing his job.

LARRY Uh, thanks?

SIX Exactly! But he's not situating his job. He is dishonest with the world, and he doesn't know his part. It's making him crazy. And so we must intervene. We must conduct an intervene-ing. An-interveen-ion. An, er, intervene-tion.

TWO An intervention?

SIX Shut up, you dummy!

PLAYERS disappear.

LARRY What the hell was that? (*Slaps himself, then roars:*) J. Lawrence Fishbein, US Embassy! (*Strides to the door of the AMBASSADOR's office*)

Act I Scene IV

American Embassy. The AMBASSADOR's Office. Nice window. Big desk. Poster of Festival. Big flag, portrait of President George W. Bush. Telephone. LARRY and AMBASSADOR. AMBASSADOR leaning back in a big chair. LARRY perched nervously on a small one.

LARRY So you see, Ambassador, we've got to call off the event as soon as possible.

AMBASSADOR Which event now, son?

LARRY The festival, sir.

AMBASSADOR The festival.

LARRY The theatre project, sir? The West Laughs! Comic Theatre Festival? Where you're giving an introduction onstage? With the Minister? In front of 5000 people? Tomorrow night?

AMBASSADOR Aha, you mean the theatre project. There's a reception, correct?

LARRY Ah. yes, sir. We've got to cancel it, sir.

AMBASSADOR Cancel the reception? This is a nation of strategic importance, son.

LARRY As I mentioned, sir, the Cultural Attachés have chosen not to participate.

AMBASSADOR Why the hell won't you all participate, son?!

LARRY Not us, Ambassador. The actors. The actors are called the Cultural Attachés. The festival has to be called off because the actors have chosen not to participate, sir.

AMBASSADOR Now slow down, son: I'm not a culture specialist.

LARRY Of course, sir. (*Very slowly.*) We have to cancel the festival because—

AMBASSADOR (*Picks up phone for no reason*) Now hold on! (*Muffles phone against his chest.*) I'm not a fool, son, and I'll thank you not to treat me like one! (*Hangs up phone with a flourish.*)

LARRY I'm sorry sir.

AMBASSADOR I'm the Extraordinary and Plenipotentiary Ambassador of the United States of America, son—

Both put their hands over their hearts and turn to the flag behind

> the AMBASSADOR's desk in deference to the words. The game runs thus: LARRY tries to keep up with the AMBASSADOR in the hand gestures his speech will necessitate. The AMBASSADOR, in turn, is an expert at this game and continually tries to trip LARRY up.

LARRY Of course, sir—

AMBASSADOR …Selected by the President (*both salute the portrait of the President*) of the United States of America (*hands over hearts, turn to flag*) to represent the security, political, and economic—

LARRY (*timidly*) And cultural, sir?

AMBASSADOR (*continues talking*) …interests of the United States of America (*hands over hearts, turn to flag*) in this sister republic (*upturned hand gesturing towards the window*); and my mandate, ratified by both houses of Congress of the United States of America (*hands*) and signed by the President of the United States of America (*salute*) neither stops at nor, candidly, contains any mention of your theatre project. My mandate from the President (*salute*) is to safeguard the vital interests of the United States of America (*hands*) in this host nation (*window*) which happens to be one of strategic importance—(*new gesture for "strategic importance": bomb falling finger movements and sounds, then explosive sound.*)

LARRY —To the—President (*salute*) of the United States of America (*hands*).

AMBASSADOR We need that airbase, son.

LARRY Respectfully, sir, I would submit that the unexpected non-place-taking of a major cultural project co-presented by the Embassy of the United States of America (*hands over hearts*) could well provoke diplomatic unpleasantness between our two (*hand on heart*) nations (*gesture towards window*) not in accordance with the spirit of your mandate from the President (*LARRY salutes*)— or the Congress… (*rapidly*) of the United States of America. In this sister republic (*hand gesture*) of strategic importance (*bomb gesture and sound effect*).

> Winded. Then they race to sit and to be the first to act as though nothing unusual has happened.

LARRY (*cont.*) To summarize, if the minister is present…nothing happens…well, it could be interpreted as a serious insult, sir.

AMBASSADOR We can't be playing that game, son.

LARRY What? But the performance—

AMBASSADOR Now slow down, son—

LARRY (*medium-slowly*) The actors aren't here, the festival cannot take place, and we've got to call it off. You have to go to the minister and tell him—

AMBASSADOR Excellent recommendation. But in this security climate—(*new gesture: machine gun*)

LARRY But now, sir, any time we speak to the ministry without cancelling we'll have to lie, sir! And then we'll look like awful fools or worse!

AMBASSADOR Well, there are different ways of framing the situation.

LARRY Sir, people are going to show up to a theatre that is in no way going to have any performers in it!

AMBASSADOR (*Into phone*) We've got to look at the opportunity cost. (*Replaces phone.*)

LARRY You have to request an audience with the minister and call it off immediately!

AMBASSADOR Request an audience? I'm not a secretary, son.

LARRY Sir, you've got to do it now!

AMBASSADOR I can assure you I will give the matter very serious consideration.

LARRY Sir, I think you're missing something—

AMBASSADOR I'll thank you not to think for me, son. It has been an absolute pleasure chatting. Door's always open. (*Door slams on LARRY.*)

LARRY What a dick!

Act I Scene V

Meeting Room at the American Embassy. CATHERINE, PIERRE-FRANÇOIS, RENATE. Radio, tuned to the BBC, is on.

BBC ANNOUNCER (*off*) In Mandijan, that Central Asian Republic's second largest city, the human rights situation is rapidly deteriorating. The Red Cross claims…

Enter LARRY. They switch off the radio.

LARRY I've been to the ambassador. And well, colleagues, it's not looking good.

PIERRE-FRANÇOIS What do you mean, looking good? Ze entire city of Mandijan is protesting on ze courthouse square, ze army is fully deployed, and we are cancelling ze performance festival!

LARRY He didn't buy it, the ambassador.

PIERRE-FRANÇOIS I am sorry, he did not buy what?

LARRY That we need to cancel the festival. Didn't buy it. And boy am I also sorry, Pierre-François.

RENATE Are you sure you presented it correctly? Maybe your sliced-up Schlange propelled your discourse into a sort of Judaistic legalism?

LARRY What???

CATHERINE How can this be? My career survived the coup in Moscow.

PIERRE-FRANÇOIS I am sorry, there is nothing to buy. The actors—

LARRY I know.

RENATE Now don't fight!

PIERRE-FRANÇOIS Are not here.

CATHERINE The bombing of Baghdad.

LARRY I know.

RENATE Stop fighting!

PIERRE-FRANÇOIS And therefore there

CATHERINE That awful year in Chad.

PIERRE-FRANÇOIS Is no festival.

LARRY I know. I said that.

RENATE We have to work together!

PIERRE-FRANÇOIS Excuse me, how could you have said that

LARRY I know.

CATHERINE The famine in Somalia.

RENATE Stop it.

LARRY I did explain.

PIERRE-FRANÇOIS How could you have explained—

CATHERINE The Bridges of Madison County—

RENATE Stop it!

PIERRE-FRANÇOIS …that there are no performers and no festival

RENATE Stop it.

CATHERINE But this—

PIERRE-FRANÇOIS And receive an answer different from

LARRY I know.

CATHERINE (*Getting weepy*) This stupid, boring city—

PIERRE-FRANÇOIS "I will call the minister immediately and explain."

LARRY Believe me.

CATHERINE (*Taking out her diplomatic accoutrements from her bag, kissing them, and laying them on the table. Diplomatic ID, diplomatic passport, fancy keys.*) My career is over.

PIERRE-FRANÇOIS Excuse me, some things clearly are not possible.

CATHERINE (*kissing the passport*) Darling Edwina, it was all for you.

RENATE (*loudly*) Stop it! Stop it! Stop fighting! This is stichomythia!

   Quiet.

LARRY What is it?

RENATE It is stichomythia. Stichomythia? Come on! You are cultural attachés!

LARRY I'm sorry. I don't know what you're talking about. I come from a country where classics aren't part of the curriculum. I'm damn sorry.

RENATE Stichomythia!

LARRY I come from a country that makes movies and Coca-Cola. How should I know from your Greco-Roman meshugoss.

RENATE Stichomythia!

PIERRE-FRANÇOIS Ah oui (*uncertain*) Stichomythie...

RENATE It is in the classical tragedy when the chorus breaks up and everybody speaks out of order. In the play it means that society is breaking up and there is no more order and there is uncertainty.

PIERRE-FRANÇOIS Ah oui.

Pause.

CATHERINE (*Suddenly angry and disdainful*) But that's obvious.

LARRY What?

CATHERINE It's fucking obvious that order is breaking down! Of course order is breaking down! And now you're coming on with this word from the Athenian tragedy just to say that order is breaking down? Order has broken down! Our careers are all bloody ruined, and all to flatter a government that ought to be isolated and shamed. Our careers are fucking over but first we have to ride the furious fucking scarlet tidal wave of haemerrhoidal shit to the rocky fucking shore. Stichomythia! Really!

PIERRE-FRANÇOIS Cherie, I know—

CATHERINE spits on PIERRE-FRANÇOIS.

LARRY Alright! All right. Let's take a moment.

PIERRE-FRANÇOIS Do not play ze peacemaker, you ignorant child.

RENATE That really was not nice, Catherine.

LARRY Everyone, please. In the interest of Democracy.

CATHERINE Democracy? I was in Berlin in '89. Democracy is nothing but a hundred D-Marks and a sticky porno arcade.

LARRY What?

CATHERINE You want stichomythia, Renate?

RENATE No!

CATHERINE Let's go.

DIPLOMATS all speak at once.

CATHERINE I have a life outside of work. But do I have a life outside of her? Is it love I'm mourning? Is it love that drags me to the brink of oblivion? Or is it lust, lust, is it your body, O holy Edwina with all your holes, is it your body that makes me despair, your body or my memory of your body, or is it you yourself or me in you or me through you? What must I be for you to save myself from the darkness, my blessed Edwina?

Even on the outs I try to maintain myself, really I do. I sleep, because if I don't sleep I won't eat and I'll likely cry and have to hide myself away and I won't be able to read my correspondence or chat with people on the telephone and I'll lose my job and go home and you'll never look at me. And then as like I'll die of some stupid accident, like being just sufficiently drunk in the presence of a potentially lethal quantity of opiate painkillers.

You're at a party, drunk on vodka and cheap champagne and you go upstairs to have a look into the loo on the off chance you feel like puking once you're in there and poke into the medicine cabinet and there it is, the stupid accident that kills you. Leaves you you know where with your head neatly thwacked against the porcelain toilet bowl before bleeding onto the pink little mat around the toilet. We're avoiding this because the whole premise is that while I'm not thriving, not husbanding a surplus of achievement satisfaction life-happiness and health still I am doing those things, and actually doing them, not neglecting those things necessary to the sustenance of life. So I'm a woman sitting on her own face, really rather contorted, really, sitting on her own face to keep her own mouth shut to prevent her from saying anything that leads around to too much health, too much unhappiness. Unstable. So how dare you even mention suicide. How dare you.

Repeat "How dare you" until all cued to stop.

PIERRE-FRANÇOIS There is a limit. There is a limit to the patience one may have. There is a limit.

In all things. I consider myself a patient man, I am loving with my friends, with my former wife, my colleagues, and also with myself. Because you must be loving with yourself to be loving with other selves—that is, other persons.

I love myself in order to love others, which I do because I am patient.

Professionally, also.

It is part of my philosophy of work always to listen to what people have to say—other people can often have interesting insights and improve your thinking on certain matters.

But there is a limit.

When one is listening, evidently, one is not speaking, and it is equally folly to act as though other persons always are right or always have correct and complete viewpoints on matters.

If one listens so much, it becomes a farce.

If one listens all the time, one almost forgets the classical, I believe it is called the golden rule:

Why do not these people listen to me? Why do not these people listen to me?

I am not here only to listen, you do not need an experienced diplomat only to listen to you, no, you presume he has some insights of value to contribute to the matter, and eventually you cease talking and listen to me. I am talking about appropriate dealings with men of experience and position—that it is I talking at this moment is not of import.

So it becomes ridiculous, all of this talking, and I do a bad service to myself and to my position and also to my partners in dialogue if I do not make clear my viewpoint and raise my voice, because my viewpoint and my voice are certainly not of lesser value than those of others. Listen to me. Listen to me. There is a limit to my patience.

Repeat "There is a limit to my patience" until all cued to stop.

LARRY J. Lawrence Fishbein, US Embassy. There's you and there's the job. J. Lawrence Fishbein, US Embassy. The job? What am I saying, the job? The career. United States Department of State, Foreign Service

The Department feeds me and clothes me—the Department gives me the use of a capacious apartment in a secure, modern building—the department gives me the use of a car and driver—the Department is like a kindly, rich uncle who's adopted me and given me the world—my Uncle Sam! And if your rich, kindly uncle adopts you and gives you the world, you're grateful, you take his name! J. Lawrence Fishbein, US Embassy. It's like the department is Julius Caesar and you're Octavian, or Augustus, or whatever.

You know, and he adopts you. Maybe it's not quite like that.

But you take his name and add it onto yours. Me and the department, J. Lawrence Fishbein, US Embassy. Me and the career.

So it's you and the career—no: career? What am I saying, career? Me and the career. It's me and the mission: no—the nation! You and the nation!

The Department of State represents the nation officially abroad—officially! Think of the honor. The United States of America is history's greatest monument to the rights of man, to the fundamental equality of each to all to each one born within the 50 states, overseas dependencies and US minor outlying islands, as well as those who have lawfully immigrated seeking freedom and fortune, and successfully acquired US nationality. Immigrants like my own grandparents, and Great Aunt Rose: my own people.

It's me and the job—no: the career—no: the mission—no: the nation. J. Lawrence Fishbein, US Embassy.

Repeat "J. Lawrence Fishbein, US Embassy" until all cued to stop.

RENATE We have to work together! We represent the ideal of the West. We have to work together.

Even if the West is capable of barbarism, like killing all the Jews, we have come up with some ideas that are important for the world. Our duty is to represent our culture here. We are not only representatives of sovereign nations—

Now it is sometimes a little hard to concentrate in the presence of Larry's cut-up Jewish dingdong. I wonder sometimes: does it get smaller if they cut it? Or does it get bigger, because of the scar tissue?

Right: focus. We are not only representatives of nations, we also represent the ideal of the west: the power of reason, beauty, and rule of law.

Consideration drives action. I do not want to make a big deal over it, because you all are making a big deal already. But...we are in a bad position. This is why we need to work together!

We have to do our jobs here and deal with our problems in a culturally adapted way. We are cultural attachés!

Judaism is fundamental to Western culture, but somehow foreign. It is very old, and points to the Eastern beginnings of our civilization.

I in-stru-men-ta-lize this knowledge of our old culture for our new culture. Modern culture. I am a cultural attaché! Reason and light. Consideration and action. Working together. The roots of our culture are in classical antiquity.

We have to do our jobs here and deal with our problems in a culturally adapted way. Modern culture. We've got to work together. We are cultural attaches!

Repeat "We've got to work together" until all cued to stop.

CATHERINE Right.

LARRY Let's take a moment. Let's get the file. Let's take a moment. Maybe there's something still that we can—

PIERRE-FRANÇOIS Excuse me, the file is useless.

LARRY I know, I know. But let's see where we stand. My mentor in the department always told me: when everything seems fucked, look through the file. I go through it from the back to the front, and put the pages in order and make it look nice, and whenever I do, I always see something that helps. It's my secret.

PIERRE-FRANÇOIS Excuse me, if you have a secret and the current situation is zis, then I am afraid your secret is worthless.

LARRY Leave if you want. I'd be happy to call a car for you. But if you want to stay, then humor me. (*Into intercom*) Hey, doll, would you mind bringing us the complete file?

EMBASSY SECRETARY (*on intercom*) Which one, Lar?

LARRY The Cultural Attachés file.

EMBASSY SECRETARY (*intercom*) You really want to look at their files in front of them, Lar?

LARRY Not these cultural attachés! The actors! The comic theatre festival!

EMBASSY SECRETARY (*intercom*) Oh, 643.21-3. Sorry!

> Door opens. EMBASSY SECRETARY gives LARRY an enormous file, and violently twits PIERRE-FRANÇOIS's nose. PIERRE-FRANÇOIS yelps. Door closes.

LARRY (*Going through file*) I tell you, there's nothing that makes me calmer than flicking these pages.

CATHERINE Unbelievable.

LARRY Ahhhhh. Oh, here's the script! Did any of you read this? ...No? No one read it?

PIERRE-FRANÇOIS I did.

CATHERINE No you didn't, you twat.

PIERRE-FRANÇOIS I read it quickly.

CATHERINE Sod off, you overblown scrotum.

PIERRE-FRANÇOIS I—skimmed it.

CATHERINE You did bloody not.

PIERRE-FRANÇOIS I read the coverage about it.

CATHERINE Stop it. Stop it. Stop it.

PIERRE-FRANÇOIS (*Timidly*) I looked at it. I am not a secretary!

    CATHERINE near tears.

LARRY (*reading*) This is something. Whoa. We are crazy—we are crazy to have hired these people.

PIERRE-FRANÇOIS My head office knows them.

CATHERINE Please, please stop.

LARRY I wonder if they read this… "Give us your piss…Even you do not deserve my shit….But it is your lumpy essence, the fruit of the world, processed and refined by your holy body…"

CATHERINE (*Laughs maniacally, understanding something.*) Of course. Of bloody course.

    RENATE goes over and reads over LARRY's shoulder.

RENATE Wow.

    RENATE reads. LARRY reads. Pause.

RENATE "Anoint us with your piss, to fortify us…"

LARRY This is really incredible.

PIERRE-FRANÇOIS Art is controversial.

CATHERINE What do you know, you dyspeptic, Rabelaisian letch.

PIERRE-FRANÇOIS (*shrinking*) I read an article about zem.

RENATE "O, please, please, I will rub it into my skin, sneak a tiny taste with the driest corner of my tongue, and then let your holy piss dry on me."

LARRY "Once it is dry, I will not let water touch my flesh until there is no shadow of the taste of your holy piss when I lick myself."

RENATE It is sort of interesting.

    LARRY laughs despite himself.

LARRY Hold on a moment—colleagues, colleagues, hold on a moment. We can go to the Deputy Minister—we can bring this to the Deputy Minister—this—

CATHERINE This filth?

LARRY Yes exactly, this filth, this piss, and tell him we think it's— morally unsuitable.

PIERRE-FRANÇOIS No: art is controversial.

CATHERINE (*In a furious rage at PIERRE-FRANÇOIS*) Carrot. Apple. Broccoli. Daikon. Turnip. Lettuce.

> *PIERRE-FRANÇOIS cowers, runs, tries to cover his ears. CATHERINE pursues him around the room, torturing him with evocations of that which he cannot digest. Simultaneous with dialogue.*

RENATE Not acceptable—

LARRY Yes, morally unsuitable, might be embarrassing, got to cancel. Do you see?

CATHERINE Tomato. Celery. Cauliflower. Asparagus.

> *PIERRE-FRANÇOIS turns to door, stops, turns back.*

PIERRE-FRANÇOIS Actually, I like asparagus.

> *EMBASSY SECRETARY opens door, stands there with the fruit basket. CATHERINE takes it, runs around tormenting PIERRE-FRANÇOIS with it. Opens a banana.*

PIERRE-FRANÇOIS Non! Par pitié!

> *CATHERINE chews and spits banana at PIERRE-FRANÇOIS, traces the path of digestion on her belly, etc.*

LARRY All right. I'll make an appointment with the Minister.

CATHERINE (*while torturing PIERRE-FRANÇOIS*) Bloody well right you will.

PIERRE-FRANÇOIS Excuse me, I believe a diplomat with more cultural experience—

CATHERINE Spinach. Broccoflower.

LARRY Who will join me? —Er, actually, Renate, are you free?

RENATE Yes, my Hebrew Warrior!

LARRY (*Brandishing a finger up in a Lenin pose*) To the Ministry!

END OF ACT ONE
INTERMISSION

Act II Scene I

Darkness. Music: "Shakin' All Over," by the Guess Who, intro repeats, no lyrics. PLAYERS, masked, dance along. LARRY walks out, music down.

SIX It's coming! It's coming!

FOUR It's coming!

TWO, THREE, FIVE It's coming!

LARRY What's coming?

FIVE The Mamamouchi!

LARRY The what?

ALL The Mamamouchi!

TWO The Mamamouchi for Larry!

TWO, THREE, FOUR, FIVE, SIX The Mamamouchi for J. Lawrence Fishbein! Mamamouchi!

SIX It's coming.

> *Music up. PLAYERS file out, each slaps LARRY on way. LARRY slaps himself.*
>
> *"Shakin' All Over." LARRY crosses to RENATE, in the lighted space. The Ministry of Information. Waiting room. LARRY, RENATE look out a large window down at the enormous, nearly empty, plan-built, megalomaniacal city.*

LARRY This is the strangest place I've served.

RENATE Every place is strange.

LARRY I guess that's true. But it's so—eerie here.

RENATE (*Going over to LARRY at the window*) Ja. It is a little uncanny.

LARRY No one on the street, the marble subway stations that are always empty, the 400-foot tall rotating bronze statue of the President—

RENATE Mann, is that something—

LARRY —And these master-planned buildings—enormous concrete slabs set down at weird angles on the steppe, like they'd been dropped from space.

RENATE Ja, dat's right: dropped from space.

LARRY And the theatre—the "Great Gathering Place of the People?"—I don't get it. It's like a tent, but it's as big as an aircraft carrier and it's covered in gold. It all kind of makes me—

RENATE puts an arm around his waist.

RENATE —Agoraphobic?

They lock eyes.

LARRY What's it all for?

Near kiss. A buzzing sound. The lights flicker for a moment and a very faint human scream is heard. Enter ASSISTANT DEPUTY MINISTER: Toupéed, with a big, Soviet-functionary mustache, glasses, and a heavy cardigan over his shirt and polyester tie. RENATE and LARRY bow.

ASSISTANT DEPUTY MINISTER You do me too much honor, Excellencies. Would you like some tea?

LARRY No thank you, Assistant Deputy Minister...is the Deputy Minister—

ASSISTANT DEPUTY MINISTER He will buzz when he is prepared to receive you. I am glad you do not wish tea. I cannot find anything these days, even the slaves—servants. Servants. This new ministry building—

RENATE It is lovely. It really fits architecturally

ASSISTANT DEPUTY MINISTER Of course!—But. These corridors are so new you cannot find your way. No doodles left by brutalized prisoners—er, long-term guests. No scratches in the wall from the—debriefings. No sign markers. No sign posts.

LARRY Uh huh (*encouraging*)

RENATE Yes.

ASSISTANT DEPUTY MINISTER No remembrances of things past.

RENATE No. Yes. It's all pretty generic.

ASSISTANT DEPUTY MINISTER No memories of—how do you put it in American? Enhanced questioning. They used to leave such nice drawings and stories, the torture victims—guests. Guests. You could remember them after they were gone. Their stories—"I miss mama." "Dasha love me forever." "Truth and love will conquer hate and lies."

RENATE Yes, that is a good one.

ASSISTANT DEPUTY MINISTER Sentimentality is charming. But the drawings were best. Sometimes even pornographic. Very nice pictures! No more, no more.

LARRY Just the wall, yes. New construction. The Embassy's that way, too.

> *Lights down, siren.* ASSISTANT DEPUTY MINISTER *sighs with pleasure.* VOICES *through bullhorns.*

VOICE (*off*) All terrorist agitators are ordered to leave the courthouse area and Timurkhabadjaladbroklakhalahova Square. Security forces are preparing comprehensive security measures.

> *Lights up.*

ASSISTANT DEPUTY MINISTER (*Purring*) Ah, the Ministry will have many new guests soon. Because of the completely justified security measures. But they go to another part of the building now.

RENATE Yes.

ASSISTANT DEPUTY MINISTER Yes. No.

LARRY No. Yes.

RENATE No. No.

ASSISTANT DEPUTY MINISTER No. But it was not always so.

LARRY No, the ministry used to be in an older building. I understand.

ASSISTANT DEPUTY MINISTER There was character and remembrances.

RENATE Yes. Is the Deputy Minister available?

ASSISTANT DEPUTY MINISTER No.

> *Buzz. Lights flicker a moment, another scream.*

RENATE Is that the buzzer?

ASSISTANT DEPUTY MINISTER No.

LARRY No?

ASSISTANT DEPUTY MINISTER No, that is not what I mean. What I mean is—I said "it was not always so."

LARRY Yes, we understand.

RENATE (*simultaneous*) The new building and the old building!

ASSISTANT DEPUTY MINISTER You would say "it was not always thus."

LARRY Why would we contradict you?

ASSISTANT DEPUTY MINISTER You misunderstand again. It must be my bad English.

LARRY Your English is astounding.

A buzzing. Lights dim. Muffled cry, off.

LARRY Is that the buzzer?

ASSISTANT DEPUTY MINISTER No. That is coming from a different part of the building.

RENATE No?

ASSISTANT DEPUTY MINISTER No. What I mean is, you would say "it was not always thus" instead of "it was not always so," no? Question of style.

RENATE Larry: stylistic question.

LARRY Ah, stylistic question. Well…I guess "thus" is slightly more formal than "so"…More…

RENATE …Literary?

LARRY Definitely more literary.

ASSISTANT DEPUTY MINISTER That is flattering.

ASSISTANT DEPUTY MINISTER sits down. Crazy, humorous beeping and buzzing.

RENATE Is that the buzzer?

ASSISTANT DEPUTY MINISTER starts vibrating and chattering over his entire body, convulsing as though he were being electrocuted. Making convulsive noises.

ASSISTANT DEPUTY MINISTER He will see you n-n-n-n-n-now.

RENATE Thank you. (*Inching away.*)

LARRY Well, it's been a pleasure.

ASSISTANT DEPUTY MINISTER D-d-d-d-d-d-d-don't touch

LARRY touches his shoulder and starts convulsing.

LARRY and ASSISTANT DEPUTY MINISTER M-m-m-m-m-m-me-me-me-me-

RENATE touches LARRY's shoulder out of concern, begins convulsing with them. HUGE GOON enters the waiting area from the DEPUTY MINISTER's office, sees the situation, slaps each of them individually, and then in a Three Stooges-style 1-2-3.

GOON Deputy Minister see you. Now.

Act II Scene II

Ministry of Information

"Shakin' All Over." As the scene opens up to reveal the DEPUTY MINISTER's office, ASSISTANT DEPUTY MINISTER picks up a pen and starts scratching on the walls. Huge, sinister portrait of the local President. RENATE and LARRY look at each other, rub their cheeks, and straighten themselves out. Large poster for the rival festival, "Remember Who Your Real Friends Are!" on an easel. DEPUTY MINISTER and comic-looking RUSSIAN, CHINESE, and IRANIAN representatives. All laugh uproariously except the CHINESE REP while removing freshly bloodied lab coats.

IRANIAN REP. (*Faux-cowering, suggesting the recently departed torture victim—er, "guest"*) "Don't hurt me! Oh mama!"

RUSSIAN REP. "It is too painful!"

DEPUTY MINISTER (*Noticing LARRY and RENATE*) Ah, it is the NATO. Your Russian, Chinese, and Iranian colleagues were just leaving, after a fruitful...conversation!

Laughter.

RUSSIAN REP. (*Playfully wagging a finger*) Now, "Remember who your real friends are," Serene Munificence!

DEPUTY MINISTER I wonder who they are?

IRANIAN REP. Here is a hint: not the Great Satan.

CHINESE REP. wordlessly hands over a red lacquered envelope.

RUSSIAN REP. Do svidanya.

DEPUTY MINISTER Do svidanya.

The DEPUTY MINISTER laughs along with them and bows slightly as they exit. REPS scowl at LARRY and RENATE as they leave. DEPUTY MINISTER stands in the threshold. LARRY and RENATE enter the office. DEPUTY MINISTER sits, looks into his envelope, pockets it, begins eating caviar straight from a tin.

DEPUTY MINISTER So sorry to keep you waiting. It is a busy time for the Ministry of Information. And we have already seen each other today.

LARRY Of course, your...

DEPUTY MINISTER raises an eyebrow, waiting for the correct title.

RENATE Serene...

LARRY Mmmmm...unificence? (*Sticks out hand*) J. Lawrence Fishbein, US Embassy.

DEPUTY MINISTER (*looks at LARRY quizzically*) Your Russian, Chinese, and Iranian friends have thoughtfully timed their festival to honor the President's birthday—the formalities: they provide such mountains of caviar. (*Keeps eating.*)

RENATE Thank you so much for making time for us again.

DEPUTY MINISTER So foolish for the European Union envoy to leave her post in protest of the completely justified security measures in response to the events at Mandijan—

LARRY (*Conciliatory*) Oh, the completely justified security measures against terrorist agitation—

DEPUTY MINISTER Exactly. We trust no other diplomatic representations will follow her example.

LARRY Yes, sir. This sister republic (*gesture*) is a nation of strategic importance (*bomb sounds and fingers*) to the President (*looks around for portrait to salute*) of the United States of America (*hand on heart. RENATE looks at him quizzically.*) You see, sir, we had a question or two about The West Laughs! Comic Theatre Festival.

DEPUTY MINISTER Really.

RENATE Yes, one or two things are not certain.

DEPUTY MINISTER Really.

LARRY Yes. And we would not want anyone to be put in an embarrassing position.

DEPUTY MINISTER I see.

LARRY The question is a bit sensitive.

DEPUTY MINISTER Really.

RENATE We need your judgment.

DEPUTY MINISTER I am a busy man.

RENATE We know—we respect that.

LARRY Your Serene Munificence, is your government really interested in our performance festival?

DEPUTY MINISTER My government has invested great resources in this partnership.

LARRY Which we appreciate tremendously, Your Serene Munificence.

RENATE But—it has come to our attention that the performers plan—

LARRY Some of their material may be a little objectionable.

DEPUTY MINISTER Really. (*Breaks the pen he is handling, tosses it furiously across the room, keeping his face calm. Buzzing. Lights dim a moment.*) There is no censorship in my country. We are committed to global cultural dialogue. I must ask to postpone the continuation of this discussion until another time.

LARRY Your Excellency—

DEPUTY MINISTER Serene Munificence!

RENATE I am sorry, Your Serene Munificence!

LARRY Would you please read just a little of this material?

>*Hands over paper.*

DEPUTY MINISTER Excuse me? You want me to read this? I am not a secretary!

RENATE It is a little obscene.

DEPUTY MINISTER I will have a look. (*DEPUTY MINISTER puts his feet up, begins to read.*) Hmm! Hmmmm. "Give us your piss." Huh! "A drop in the eye."

LARRY You see, Serene Munificence?

DEPUTY MINISTER I will never understand some things about the West.

RENATE We are sorry.

>*DEPUTY MINISTER starts to chuckle.*

DEPUTY MINISTER "Asparagus!"

>*The storm gathers, and he laughs with an open throat. Wears himself out.*

DEPUTY MINISTER (*cont.*) There is no censorship in my country. My government intends to corroborate its excellent relations with all nations of the world, especially given the misunderstanding regarding the ongoing events at Mandijan. Thank you for your visit. I look forward to the premiere. Tomorrow, isn't it?

>*DEPUTY MINISTER and office disappear: white curtains fall. LARRY and RENATE alone in the white space.*

RENATE I think we are in trouble. How do we get out of here, anyway?

LARRY I—I don't know. (*Stricken. Panic attack.*) We're trapped. My god, we're prisoners. I can't breathe. I'm in danger.

> *SIX comes out with huge powder pouf, hits LARRY in the face with it and exits. "Shakin' All Over" starts low and crescendos.*

LARRY (*cont.*) There aren't any windows here. (*Feels way along walls.*) No way out. I'm trapped. Please. Help me. Take me to the embassy. (*Kneels, lies on the floor. Yells.*) How do we get out of here? Please. Where's the car. Please. I can't breathe. Please. (*Grabs RENATE's knees.*) This is serious!

Act II Scene III

Music out. Dark. VOICE through bullhorns, off.

VOICE (*off*) In reaction to the arson at Mandijan, the perimeter of Timurkhabadjaladbroklakhalahova Square has been sealed. Security forces are moving on the courthouse. Curfew in effect immediately. Nationwide.

The American Embassy: LARRY's Apartment.

Mostly bare, generic room. A portrait of JFK, the poster for the festival, and a large, child's poster of Ancient Rome. LARRY and RENATE entering through the door.

LARRY Thanks for seeing me home. I don't know what happened there.

RENATE (*Fishing something out of her purse.*) Here, Larry, you should take this lozenge. You are not well.

LARRY So kind of you to notice! I am feeling a little piqued.

RENATE A little piqued? You are joking, Larry. You just had a complete panic attack at the Ministry of Information. Take it.

LARRY Why not. (*Takes it. Pause.*) Strong herbal flavor in this lozenge.

RENATE Yes, it is homeopathic. Larry, we are going to have sex.

LARRY (*Grabbing for her breast*) Well if it's that kind of party...

RENATE (*Slapping his hand away playfully*) But not yet. First you listen, then we talk. Then we do a sex act.

RENATE looks at LARRY, who slowly starts extending his hand towards her breast.

RENATE (*cont.*) Exactly—but not yet. (*pause*) It is from the Netherlands, the lozenge.

LARRY Fine pharmaceutical tradition in the Netherlands. (*Sucks awkwardly on the lozenge.*)

RENATE Listen. Larry, you are afraid of going mad, yes? (*LARRY staring at her breasts.*) Larry! You are afraid of madness, yes?

LARRY Craziness? I guess I am.

RENATE Why?

LARRY My aunt and uncle are crazy.

RENATE They let two crazies marry?

LARRY No, my mother's sister and brother.

RENATE Crazy how?

LARRY Throwing-stuff crazy, pulling-your-teeth-out-because-of-the-radio-signals crazy.

RENATE What do they have?

LARRY Oh, general crazy. Paranoid schizophrenia. State hospital.

RENATE Listen: I am not a doctor but you don't have that.

LARRY No?

RENATE Do you hear voices?

LARRY Absolutely not! Absolutely not!

RENATE (*wary*) Okay…

LARRY But enough about me. Can we get to the sex act already?

Reaches for breast. RENATE slaps hand away.

RENATE Not yet. Now, what about going mad, or "crazy", are you afraid of?

LARRY Just being crazy; being out of control—like just now at the ministry.

RENATE But you are in control now?

LARRY The job gives me control.

RENATE So what is control?

LARRY Ah—keeping it together. Presenting myself correctly. As a Foreign Service Officer.

RENATE So control is the job. And it's also how you keep the job. And it's also how you stay sane. If you are sane.

LARRY Oh, man, no, control is—it's—being able to do the job. But wait—I'm being selfish. It's not a job, it's a career—I mean, it's not a career, it's a mission: the nation! Wait, the mission isn't the nation, it's Democracy! (*Rubs down his face with both hands, a la Curly Fine*) Gimme! (*Reaches for breast. She slaps his hand away.*)

RENATE Okay, Larry, so Democracy is control?

LARRY Yes!—No! Democracy is Freedom!

RENATE Freedom from madness?

LARRY Yes—

RENATE So Democracy is Freedom. Freedom is Freedom from Madness, and Freedom from Madness is control.

LARRY Yes—no! Control is freedom.

RENATE That sounds pretty confused, doesn't it, Larry.

LARRY Look—Renate—the job keeps me sane. But also—

RENATE If you go insane you lose the job; if you lose the job you go insane. I am going to help you, Larry. I had a professor once. He said that the western culture, the idea of the West was built on three hills. Listen: There is first the Acropolis in Athens, which stands for reason and grace. You know, classical beauty: the deep symmetry of design, the effortless repose of the sculptures. Are you following, Larry?

LARRY Acropolis, grace and reason.

RENATE Very good! (*Larry reaches for breast, she slaps away more playfully*) Almost there. Second is the Temple Mount in Jerusalem. This gave us faith and sacrifice. The gift of Jesus and the hope of resurrection. You understand this importance in our culture.

LARRY But I'm Jewish.

RENATE And I can't vait to see your ritually mutilated Zauberstab.

LARRY Thanks?

RENATE But trust me, you're a westerner first.

LARRY I'm not from the west; I'm from Connecticut.

RENATE Westerner like The West, Larry. Like NATO. Trust me. We're almost to the fun part. (*Slaps away LARRY's hand*) No, Larry. So: Temple Mount.

LARRY Faith.

RENATE Yes. And sacrifice.

LARRY So what's the third hill?

RENATE Larry! It's right behind you.

> LARRY *turns around, turns back quizzically. Reaches for breast.*

RENATE (*cont.*) No, Larry. On your little poster. The Capitoline Hill in Rome. What does that stand for?

LARRY Greatness?

RENATE No, Larry. The Capitoline Hill stands for law and order.

LARRY Huh.

RENATE And something else.

LARRY What?

RENATE Control.

LARRY Whoa. What?

RENATE Power and enforcement and the clarity of the law. Look at those buildings, Larry! Power! The West—

LARRY The West…But wait—where does the comedy come in?

RENATE Comedy?

LARRY Comedy: The West Laughs!, right? Which of your verkakte hills is Comedy?

RENATE Oh, Larry. The comedy is trying to reconcile them all. (*Pause. LARRY scratches his head.*) Do you feel like you understand the job better now?

LARRY No. Maybe? No.

RENATE Our culture demands reason and grace, faith and sacrifice, and legal control. How do all these fit together? How do you build something on three hills?

LARRY Uh—

RENATE Exactly. Only a madman would put these values together.

LARRY But—

RENATE But you are afraid of madness, I know. Listen, Larry: you must make madness part of your act.

LARRY What act?

RENATE Just as the West needs comedy to reconcile its impossible values, so every diplomat needs an act.

LARRY What's your act?

RENATE I am a deceptively intelligent (*Sticks out her breasts towards him*) sex-crazed ingénue.

LARRY Huh! (*Reaches for breast. She lets it stay there a moment.*)

RENATE Yes. And you are mad.

LARRY Great.

RENATE But you only act mad, and that way you stay sane! Get it?

LARRY No.

RENATE Don't worry, you will. That lozenge I gave you?

LARRY Yes?

RENATE It was hashish.

LARRY Hashish?!?! (*Quickly withdraws hand from breast, wipes his brow*) Now I'm really gonna be meshuggeh!

RENATE (*Up against LARRY*) Don't worry about it, Schatzi! Now we get to act!

>They begin groping. RENATE undoes her shirt, LARRY, getting increasingly stoned, begins to fumble with his pants, but has difficulty. As they wrangle together, TWO, FOUR, FIVE, SIX appear onstage, masked.

LARRY Wait a minute—

TWO Give us your piss, Larry!

RENATE Ach Larry, the historical trauma of your people—

FOUR Mystical essence of asparagus, Larry!

LARRY I haven't had asparagus since Thanksgiving!

RENATE What?

LARRY Nothing.

RENATE The physical trauma of your penis—

FIVE Ooh!

RENATE It is all one beautifully scarred oneness!

SIX Mamamouchi, Larry.

RENATE Talk to me in Jewish, my little rabbi.

LARRY Jewish? Wait a minute—uh… (*uncertainly sings the refrain of the Passover Four Questions*) "Ma nishtana halayla hazeh…"

RENATE What does that mean?

LARRY Uh, "Why is this night different from all other nights?"

RENATE Oh ja, ja! Now show me the covenant of Abraham.

TWO, FOUR, FIVE, SIX It's coming, Larry.

RENATE (*Feels in his pants*) Ach nein, Larry—dein Schwanz, it is not—

TWO, FOUR, FIVE, SIX MAMAMOUCHI, LARRY!

>LARRY and RENATE stop making out. LARRY is weeping with frustration. PLAYERS point and laugh, then split. RENATE stares at him. Needless to say, LARRY is freaking out.

LARRY The piss—the actors—asparagus—Mama?

RENATE Where the hell did that come from?

LARRY It definitely wasn't the voices in my head!

RENATE Uh-oh.

LARRY What? (*getting antsy*) Ah—can I offer you anything? Glass of water? Cheese and crackers? Coca-Cola? Glass of wine? Dude: Wine. Wine would be really good. Oh—but I—I don't want to go into the kitchen. It's weird out there.

RENATE Yes it is.

LARRY Oh, man. I'm scared.

RENATE (*Hugs him*) (*Aside*) The lozenge might have been a mistake.

LARRY Can we go to sleep?

RENATE I doubt it.

LARRY I can't handle it. Wine! Get the wine. Please, please get the wine!

RENATE (*Getting up*) Where is it?

LARRY In the refrigerator.

RENATE Where are the glasses.

LARRY I don't know. Give me the wine.

> *RENATE brings the wine bottle over to LARRY, on the bed. He drinks a whole lot of it.*

RENATE (*Packing her things.*) I hope you learned something. I'm leaving, Larry.

> *EMBASSY SECRETARY appears.*

EMBASSY SECRETARY I wouldn't recommend that, hon.

LARRY & RENATE Aaah!

EMBASSY SECRETARY Evening, y'all!

LARRY Hi.

RENATE Em, why can't I leave?

LARRY (*Looks around, takes a big slug of wine*) Um…

EMBASSY SECRETARY Well, there's alarms, paperwork…

> *LARRY passes RENATE the bottle. She drinks.*

RENATE Ach, Americans.

LARRY (*Taking wine back*) Oh, um, curfew too.

EMBASSY SECRETARY (*exiting*) That's right, hon. Now night night, y'all!

LARRY Um, night.

RENATE Vat de hell was dat?

LARRY What? Oh, her? That's nothing. It's the piss guys that really scare me.

RENATE What is it with you and piss, Larry?

LARRY Wait a minute…piss…meshugoss…order…festival…Whoah.

RENATE He is going within.

LARRY So you're saying…

RENATE Yes?

LARRY So you're saying that what our culture wants from us is crazy?

RENATE In a way.

LARRY And we're always gonna fail at it?

RENATE Sort of.

LARRY So either we laugh at culture and pretend to be nuts or else we take it seriously and really go nuts?

RENATE Well…

LARRY That's it. I got it.

RENATE I'm not quite sure—

LARRY We'll put the damn festival on ourselves if we have to!

RENATE Larry, you are being crazy!

LARRY Crazy is as crazy does. I want my marbles back!

RENATE This is not what I meant!

LARRY God bless America! To the theatre, Renate!

RENATE But the curfew—

LARRY Damn the curfew! Damn these fascists! You call the others; I'll get the armored limo.

LARRY struggles into a white, ankle-length nightshirt.

RENATE Whoa, nice nightshirt!

LARRY (*Into intercom*) Call the driver and bring me the complete file—643.21-3. Now! (*to RENATE*) We're going to the theatre! To the Great Gathering Place of the People!

Interlude 2

Bare stage. TWO, THREE, FOUR, FIVE, SIX, masked. LARRY walks on...

FOUR Is this wrong? I kind of feel for him!

LARRY Yes!

SIX Is what wrong?

TWO The horrific stress we're subjecting him to?

SIX I wouldn't say so.

LARRY I am extremely pissed off at you guys!

TWO That nightshirt?

FOUR Ooh, let's put on a nightcap too!

SIX Great idea! (*Puts a nightcap on LARRY.*)

FIVE The (*limp hand gesture*) droop in his (*vulgar hand gesture*) dingdong? Heh heh.

THREE Well nothing new there!

LARRY Hey!

FIVE Or the horrible, brain-stewing lesson we're going to inflict on him?

LARRY Please no more brain-stewing!

SIX Oh, come on! Weaklings! We are fighting for the light, for the comic disposition that is the only thing that enables human life for more than two seconds! People! You disgust me! Is this the allegiance you show to the just cause?

TWO Well, I guess you're right.

FOUR But those tears were real—

LARRY There weren't any tears!

TWO So what if they were?

SIX Yeah. You wanna see real tears?

FOUR Uh—

SIX Watch this. (*to FIVE*) You're an idiot. You're stupid, and you're old.

Slaps TWO. TWO pretends to cry, then slaps SIX. FIVE slaps SIX. FOUR slaps SIX. SIX begins to cry.

FOUR I see. Is that a metaphor?

SIX (*crying*)   No. Nobody understands me.

LARRY (*Singing, uncertainly*) Mah nishtanah halaylah hazeh…

Act III Scene I

Dark. VOICES through bullhorns.

VOICE (*off*) Informational support to terrorist agitation will not be tolerated.

OTHER VOICE (*off*) Tyrant!

Shots fired.

VOICE (*off*) Foreign journalists must leave the republic effective immediately.

OTHER VOICE (*off*) Down with the Tyrant!

Explosion.

VOICE (*off*) Remain calm. Security measures are proceeding.

> *Great Gathering Place of the People. Dark. Echo. Enter LARRY, wearing a nightshirt and now a nightcap, carrying his briefcase. Enter RENATE.*

LARRY A little eerie here.

RENATE I'm going to—Hey, Larry! Nice cap!

LARRY (*Feels head*) Oh, um, thanks.

RENATE Where did you get that?

LARRY Not sure.

RENATE Larry, stay here. I'm going to look for Pierre-François and Catherine.

> *RENATE exits.*

LARRY Oh no, it's starting, the panic. Oh boy. Hmm hmm hmm. I might vomit. Where's the exit? I'll feel better if I just know I could find it if I needed to. So many hallways—I don't remember how we got here. (*Sees a lit candle. Takes it.*) Oh, here's a candle. (*Candle illuminates spear carrier-type GUARD.*) Aaaah! (*To GUARD*) Excuse me—where's the exit?

> *Silence.*

LARRY (*cont.*) Exit? Ex-It? Um—"vykhod?"

GUARD (*Blows out candle*) No exit.

LARRY No exit?

> *SIX appears, dressed as a circus impresario, with red riding coat and whip.*

SIX All hail. We are those players that have been sent for by His Imperial Excellency the American Ambassador. (*Courtly bow.*)

LARRY Excuse me?

SIX Might you be Lawrence, the attaché culturel?

LARRY I might?

SIX I've brought you flowers. (*Flowers.*)

LARRY But you—

SIX One of the players, Excellency! The comic players. For whom you sent. We've arrived. We're ready to perform. As requested.—Are you all right?

LARRY But—players?—(*Starts awkwardly searching in his briefcase*) You sent a letter. It's in the file. You…canceled. Your letter—

SIX Letter? What letter?

LARRY The letter—

SIX The letter?

LARRY It's in the file!—About the cloak of…jollity.

SIX Oh, that letter! That was a ruse. Good one, eh?

LARRY What? (*Pinches himself. Looks around. Sticks hand out*) J. Lawrence Fishbein, US Embassy. (*SIX looks at LARRY's outstretched hand.*)–But then—but—where are the rest of you?

SIX Oh, don't worry: you'll be seeing us! I have to go.

LARRY You have to go? Wait! So you'll do the reception?

> *SIX disappears into the darkness. Comes back to give him more flowers. Disappears.*

LARRY Am I hallucinating? Am I that stoned? t*To GUARD*) Did you see that? (*Silence*)

GUARD No exit.

> *LARRY looks at flowers. THREE enters. FIVE in the shadow.*

LARRY Thank heavens, Renate! Have you seen the—people? The—performers?

THREE (*No accent*) We are poor players, most high Excellency, gratified to be of service to you.

> *LARRY jumps and yelps. FIVE emerges from shadow.*

FIVE The honor, Your Excellency, of presenting the humor of the occident for the pleasure of this immensely forceful people's dictatorship...(*Courtly bow.*)

THREE The honor is not lost on us, Excellency. (*Courtly curtsey.*)

LARRY You're not Renate....(*to FIVE*) but you too—you look like—

FIVE Surely, you're confusing us with someone else.

THREE What an honor to feel familiar to you, Excellency!

LARRY But what about the letter in the file?

THREE Letter? What letter?

FIVE What do the letters matter, Excellency, when it's the words that count. (*Stupefied reaction from LARRY*) And may I say, nice cap!

LARRY I'm sorry. I'm very very sorry. Just a moment. (*Shakes his head rapidly, tries to pull himself together.*) I'm just—a bit confused. (*Extends hand.*) J. Lawrence Fishbein, US Embassy. Very, very, very pleased to make your acquaintance. Just hold on a moment; my colleagues, the cultural attachés, the other cultural attachés—the other other cultural attachés—will be along any second.

FIVE Excuse us, we have to go.

LARRY You have to go now?

THREE We'll be right back.

> *THREE and FIVE disappear into the darkness.*

LARRY Hello?

> *LARRY looks at flowers. Looks at GUARD. No response.*

> *THREE comes back and hands him flowers, kisses him, giggling. Disappears once more. LARRY looks at the GUARD.*

LARRY No exit?

> *GUARD shakes his head. Enter CATHERINE and PIERRE-FRANÇOIS.*

PIERRE-FRANÇOIS Lawrence, we are here.

LARRY Okay. Hello. Pleasure. I get it. You're players. You didn't send a letter, but we got one anyway, or else it was a ruse. You're ready to perform and you're going to give me flowers. (*Extends hand.*) J. Lawrence Fishbein, US Embassy.

CATHERINE (*Slaps him.*) Larry! What the bloody hell are you on about? Why did you call us here? The streets are completely bloody empty because of the curfew. Tanks everywhere. It feels like the bloody Reichstag just burned!

PIERRE-FRANÇOIS The Ministry car followed us all the way. Zey are going to arrest us. You have gone crazy!

LARRY They're—

CATHERINE And what the hell are you doing in that cap?

PIERRE-FRANÇOIS Speak, man! Zis is an outrage! Do you know what time it is? I am not a secretary!

LARRY (*Draws a deep breath, holds it, extends hand*) J. Lawrence Fishbein, US Embassy. I'm terribly sorry to have disturbed you so late in the evening, but I fear

CATHERINE Speak, man! Enough with the pleasantries!

PIERRE-FRANÇOIS Speak, Larry, zis is impossible.

LARRY Colleagues, I'm frightfully sorry—

CATHERINE & PIERRE-FRANÇOIS Speak, man!

LARRY J. Lawrence Fishbein, US Embassy.

CATHERINE He's snapped. Larry (*Slap*) why have you called us here?

LARRY Oh. Right. Sorry. They're here.

PIERRE-FRANÇOIS Who's here?

LARRY The Cultural Attachés.

CATHERINE (*Slap*) We're here because you called us here, you lunatic!

LARRY Ow! Colleagues! We have to—

CATHERINE Larry, you're in shock. (*Slap.*) You're hysterical. (*Slap.*) You've got to compose yourself. (*Slap.*) And where's your little girlfriend?

> CATHERINE *slaps* LARRY. PIERRE-FRANÇOIS *slaps* LARRY. CATHERINE *slaps* PIERRE-FRANÇOIS. PIERRE-FRANÇOIS *raises his hand towards* CATHERINE.

CATHERINE Don't you dare.

LARRY Stop it, colleagues! This is stichomythia!

> RENATE *pokes her head in.*

RENATE Stichomythia?

PIERRE-FRANÇOIS Again?

CATHERINE I'm the lady sitting on her face so sometimes I have to speak, and accurately and quickly and productively, too, when my arse is literally parked directly upon my face and my back's about to give out, obviously.

In these situations I am generally able to move my arse aside in concert with the movement of my lips, jaws, throat etcetera in speech, and also to move the buttocks while I speak, to enable speaking, to keep the job, to enable sleep and life, and the voice that emanates sounds composed and intelligent enough to distract attention from the fact that it arose through an acrobatically gesticulating, properly verbal, engaged arse. Mouth wrestling with arse. Voice wrestling with arse. Arse repressing mouth. Arse repressing voice.

Repeat until cued to stop.

PIERRE-FRANÇOIS There is a limit. For perhaps I may submit that sometimes my viewpoint and my voice might be of greater value than others. Quite often of greater value, even.

The fact that my partners in dialogue do not recognize or foresee this causes me indeed some personal discord, not that it need be personal to be of value, or valued, am I not right?

It is my job to speak my opinions and to be respected, I am an official representative of a sovereign nation, it is not vain but rather practical and unavoidable for me to say, I am sorry, but please listen to me. Listen to me.

I am an official representative of a sovereign nation, of the mirror of the world, of the French Republic, and my voice must be heard, do you hear me?

Repeat until cued to stop.

LARRY And so you're working for democracy, you're part of democracy, it's you and democracy, and then you maybe sometimes work with nations that aren't exactly democracies—J. Lawrence Fishbein, US Embassy—but that assist our enforcement of global order—I mean our global enforcement of orderçI mean global security—I mean democracy—and if these governments maybe sometimes, occasionally, kind of implement security measures that maybe kind of look a teensy little bit like brutally repressive massacres of unarmed protesters…What's the alternative? I mean are we supposed to let the terrorists win? I mean, global security, I mean democracy, I mean J. Lawrence Fishbein, US Embassy. US Embassy, J. Lawrence Fishbein.

Repeat until cued to stop.

RENATE We have to work together! We represent the ideal of the West. Wiener have to work together. I mean we have to work together.

Even if the West is capable of barbarism, like killing all the Jews with their big, circumcised peninses, we have come up with some ideas that are important for the world. Our duty is to represent our culture here. We are not only representatives of sovereign nations—

We represent the crazy ideals of the west: the power of reason, beauty, and rule of law.

I do not want to make a big deal over it, because you all are making a big deal already. But…we are in a bad position, you know? This is why we need to work together!

Repeat until cued to stop.
RENATE disappears.

CATHERINE Right.

LARRY LISTEN TO ME! They're here! The actors! The actors are here!

CATHERINE &PIERRE-FRANÇOIS What? The comic players?

LARRY Yes! The comic players. (*Stops short, starts to recognize something.*) The Cultural Attachés. They're—here.

CATHERINE Here? But the letter—

LARRY They're here; they said the letter was only a ruse—

PIERRE-FRANÇOIS A ruse?

LARRY A ruse—and they're going to do the reception.

PIERRE-FRANÇOIS Mon Dieu, zis is perfect! Ze reporters are banished and ze players are here? O Genève, city of peace and melted cheese, you are mine. Take zat, you irritating François-Pierre!

CATHERINE Merciful heavens! If the festival is on—then I'll make it out of this shithole alive! Edwina, my love…

PIERRE-FRANÇOIS Take a breath, Larry. We leave the room for a moment.

Offers his arm to CATHERINE.

LARRY No, they'll be right back. They—said they'd be right back.

CATHERINE (*leaving, takes PIERRE-FRANÇOIS's arm*) Take a breath, Larry. (*To PIERRE-FRANÇOIS*) Excuse me.

Goes back and slaps LARRY once more. Returns to PIERRE-FRANÇOIS, takes his arm, leaves with him. As they exit:

CATHERINE Edwina, darling, put your red dress on. London, here I come!

PIERRE-FRANÇOIS Ah, Happiness: have you other home but Europe?

Exit CATHERINE & PIERRE-FRANÇOIS.

LARRY Where are you going? But these flowers! (*LARRY looks again at flowers, at GUARD. To GUARD*) You see these flowers, don't you?

GUARD No exit.

LARRY The comedians are here, we're saved, it's the middle of the night in the theatre and there are state security agents throughout the building and there's a nationwide curfew and the performance is tomorrow and the minister's coming and he's the president's brother and they want me to breathe? (*Pant, pant, pant*) J. Lawrence Fishbein, US Embassy. US Embassy, J. Lawrence Fishbein.

Enter FOUR with TWO, who is dressed like a baby.

LARRY Thank goodness you've come to your senses! (*Notices baby attire*) Um—

TWO Larry?

LARRY Yes!

TWO The dame with the rack said you were looking for us.

FOUR Now that's no way to speak to our host! Your Excellency—

LARRY Oy vey.

TWO The dame with the rack said you were looking for us, host. Say, that's some headgear!

FOUR Very fetching, Your Excellency…

LARRY Players? Comic players?

FOUR The same, Excellency. Why, look at us…what else could we be?

TWO She's saying: look at the talking baby with the foul mouth and the drinking problem.

FOUR It's part of the act. Drinking problems are funny, you see, but mostly with babies.

SIX (*entering*) Well, we all have drinking problems and we're all funny.

LARRY Hello again?

FIVE (*off*) I wouldn't go that far.

SIX On a good night, well, comrades, I would. Oh, I just adore that hat!

TWO Nah, maybe we're confident, but that prostitute is never competent.

FIVE (*enters*) You mean concomitant.

SIX What?

TWO That's not what I mean at all!

LARRY (*to FIVE*) Hello again?

TWO Listen: I said competent, meaning funny. I said, she (*pointing to FOUR*) was never, never, never competent. Even when she was young during the Eisenhower Administration.

FOUR Well I never! I was young during the Reagan Administration!

TWO I guess fifty's still young. Here's some flowers.

SIX Those flowers were for our host.

TWO It's ok. We got a value pack.

LARRY Value pack?

TWO Here, here's some other ones.

FOUR Now now, that's not how we speak to our host!

TWO Here's some other ones, host.

THREE (*entering*) We're very happy to be here, Excellency.

LARRY You wouldn't happen to be the German cultural attaché, would you?

THREE What was that, Excellency?

LARRY Hello again?

TWO That's BS.

THREE We're moderately happy to be here.

TWO Warmer.

THREE We're not so hot on being here.

TWO Give the lassie a prize.

FIVE Now, now, now! We must not be ungrateful! Our host is welcoming us to this shit country! Heh heh.

FOUR Aren't you, Excellency?

TWO He hasn't been too welcoming.

FOUR Well I'm certain he will be.

SIX And he'll be less and less welcoming the more you all speak to him like that!

FIVE Your Excellency, I must apologize for my colleagues.

SIX Comic performers quite frequently lose sight of manners, you see: we have a different, less permanent view of social affairs.

THREE This lecture again? Excellency, I'm telling you, this one is the Comrade Trotsky of comic players.

TWO She's a comic-ist. We call her Comrade Schlocksky.

SIX Don't call me that! We don't do schlock!

LARRY Less permanent how?

TWO Like the damage we do don't last forever if it's funny.

LARRY And if it isn't funny?

TWO Well, then we make it funny for ourselves.

SIX As long as one of us is suffering, Excellency, the rest of us can laugh.

FOUR And if all of us are suffering, then we can laugh at the one who's suffering most.

FIVE And the one who's suffering most can laugh with us. Or if he

FOUR Or she

FIVE Is feeling more philosophical, then he

FOUR Or she

FIVE Can laugh at us.

LARRY How do they laugh at you if they're suffering worst?

SIX They laugh at us for lacking the moral vision to see their suffering.

LARRY I see…Wait, what the hell is going on here?

FIVE We've got to go.

LARRY You've got to go? Wait just a minute, let me call my friends, they'd love to meet you.

TWO We, uh, we got to go.

LARRY But where on earth would you…

> *They leave. LARRY lets out a little yelp of confusion.*

LARRY (*Calling after*) What, no flowers?

> *THREE scurries back and brings him flowers. Kisses him. Giggles. Exits again. Pause. LARRY bites off the head of a flower and spits it on the floor. Throws down the rest. Starts to trample them. RENATE enters.*

LARRY (*Irritated*) What, you want me to thank you for the flowers?

RENATE Larry! What is wrong with you? (*Slap. LARRY yelps again.*) You told Catherine and Pierre-François the actors are here? You have lost it! I should not have given you the medicine. Now you will be crazy forever. And you were so cute! (*Cries on his shoulder. Rapidly recovers.*) I must go now.

> *Runs away crying.*

LARRY She has to go. Everyone has to go. They're in a locked government theatre in a hostile dictatorship on the Eurasian steppe in the middle of a human rights disaster. Of course they have to go. (*To GUARD*) Right? (*GUARD nods "no" again. Not amused.*)

COMIC PLAYERS enter.

LARRY Finally, there you are! My colleague was just here! Where the hell did you go?

FIVE Oh, we had to step out.

FOUR To check on something.

SIX Now to business. We're here, we're ready to perform. We hope our little joke made an impression—

LARRY What did you have to check on just now?

FIVE What does it matter?

TWO We were checking on ze—rigging.

LARRY Did you say—"zee" rigging?

TWO Yes, ze rigging. I mean no. Damn it.

LARRY Zee rigging?

SIX Ah—we need to go again.

LARRY But the diplomats!

ALL Bye bye!

Exit all save LARRY, GUARD.

LARRY This is—outrageous. An insult. Who do they think I am, a secretary?

Interlude 3

COMIC PLAYERS onstage.

SIX Well, this is it. This is it. The lesson, the denouement.

THREE Time to be serious, eh, Comrade Schlocksky?

SIX Don't call me that!

TWO Serious as a—

SIX For the love of Groucho, do not say it.

FIVE Heart attack?

Slaps all around, converging on FIVE.

FIVE (*Clutches heart, convulses, grunts*) Uh—ah—uh—I'm really not feeling—

SIX Oh, shut up. Let's get on with it. Are we all present?

TWO Are we all present? You shut up!

> *FIVE collapses.*

SIX All present. Check your props and watch your cues. Get up, Five!

FIVE No! I'm having a—

> *More slaps.*

SIX All right: Merde. Let us begin. (*Calls backstage to LARRY.*) You hear that, Larry?

LARRY (*off, uncertainly*) I'm not a secretary?

FIVE (*still collapsed onstage*) Help…

> *FIVE is dragged off.*

ALL PLAYERS Merde!

Act III Scene II.

The Investiture of the Mamamouchi.

Great Gathering Place of the People

LARRY is pushed onstage. RENATE is in the house. Enter AMBASSSADOR in the first row of the orchestra.

LARRY Ambassador! Ah—Ambassador...I have no idea what's going on here, but things are extremely hairy and I urge you to return to the Embassy immediately.

Actors come out and place table, chairs, water glasses and pitchers, and a portrait of the US President on the stage.

AMBASSADOR Son...this is a delicate situation. Let's try to concentrate. (*Whispers*) Are you on drugs, son?

LARRY N-no, sir! (*Sticks out hand*) J. Lawrence Fishbein, US Embassy!

AMBASSADOR Hmm. Have a glass of water, Fishbein.

AMBASSADOR and RENATE walk up onstage. LARRY is pushed into a very short chair. He starts drinking water out of sheer confusion and doesn't stop throughout this scene until the water's gone.

AMBASSADOR (*cont.*) Miss, can you brief me—rapidly?

RENATE Well, Mr. Ambassador, if I may—

AMBASSADOR Please, sit.

AMBASSADOR pushes in her chair.

RENATE (*sits*) Thank you. There are a couple of concerns.

AMBASSADOR Uh-huh.

RENATE and AMBASSADOR remove notebooks. LARRY pauses his water drinking to remove the enormous file from his briefcase. Puts it on the table.

AMBASSADOR (*to LARRY*) Glad you're prepared, son.

SIX appears from nowhere behind LARRY and puts a tie loosely around his neck.

AMBASSADOR Wait—Fishbein, you're sitting down to negotiations looking like that? (*beat*) Straighten your tie.

LARRY automatically adjusts his tie, then looks down, sees it, and shrieks. AMBASSADOR motions SIX to sit.

SIX Thank you for inviting me to sit in.

AMBASSADOR Of course, Miss. (*to RENATE*) So:

RENATE Vell, regarding de performers. First they said they would come to do the festival—

AMBASSADOR And reception.

RENATE Correct, and reception; then they said they wouldn't do the reception, then they said they would not come at all, then they showed up, and now according to Larry they keep disappearing.

AMBASSADOR (*Taking a note*) Uh-huh. Noted.

RENATE Okay, moving on…the content of the performance pieces is actually really weird—

AMBASSADOR Subjectively.

RENATE Vell, ja, subjectively. But it is very, em, sadistic and scatological.

> *LARRY downs a big glass of water.*

AMBASSADOR (*Taking a note*) "…and scatological." Okay.

RENATE Next, de somewhat bigger issue, which is—why are we doing a major cultural project with this government at all? The security response to the events at Mandijan is really quite—objectionable. Do we really want to be working with them at all now?

AMBASSADOR (*Taking a note*) Aaand the question of optics.

RENATE Shouldn't we be registering a complaint instead?

AMBASSADOR Got it. Was that all from your side?

RENATE I believe so, yes. Oh, wait: also, Larry took an overdose of hashish and now probably he is permanently deranged.

AMBASSADOR (*Takes a note*) Fishbein deranged. Got it. Let's bracket that one for the moment. Is that all your points?

RENATE (*Checks through her list*)—For the moment, yes, Mr. Ambassador.

AMBASSADOR All right. Let me address your issues in order, if I may. Performers: here, not here, say they won't perform, disappear. (*To SIX*) You're here now.

SIX Yes, sir.

AMBASSADOR You'll be here tomorrow night.

SIX Yes, sir.

AMBASSADOR You'll perform.

SIX Yes, sir.

AMBASSADOR Then that issue seems resolved.—Oh, this is serious: you threatened not to show up at the reception? That's a red line for us.

SIX Oh, that was taken out of context, Your Excellency.

AMBASSADOR You'll be at the reception.

SIX Of course.

AMBASSADOR (*Crossing out a line in his notebook*) And—good. So, moving on.

RENATE Content.

AMBASSADOR Right, content. "Really weird," "sadistic," "scatological." (*to SIX*) Now—is that a fair characterization of your material, ma'am?

SIX Absolutely, Excellency.

AMBASSADOR Any chance of your toning it down?

SIX With all due respect, Your Imperial Excellency, Western comedy is sadistic and scatological.

AMBASSADOR I see your point.

SIX And Democracy has nothing to apologize for.

AMBASSADOR Agreed. Good with me. You got a note on that, Fishbein?

LARRY Um—Democracy?

AMBASSADOR (*To RENATE*) Good with you, Miss?

RENATE I guess so?

AMBASSADOR Good with you, Fishbein? Great. (*Crosses out line*) Now. On to your so-called bigger problem, which if I understand correctly is the optics of doing the festival at all given the (*Machine gun gesture*) current security climate.

RENATE Ja.

AMBASSADOR Let me share the American perspective. (*cracks his knuckles*) Regardless of its domestic policies, this government is a (*hand gesture behind him*)

LARRY Sister republic—

AMBASSADOR That's right, Fishbein, and a friend of democracy in very unstable times. And all friends of democracy can count on the steadfast support of the United States of America. And its European allies. (*Fixes RENATE with his gaze*) Would you agree with that, Miss?

RENATE (*after a beat*) Yes, Ambassador.

AMBASSADOR (*Crossing out line*) The festival is an apolitical gesture of that friendship. Great. Productive talks! Okay: and finally—why we don't lodge a complaint with the government about the (*bomb dropping, gun shooting finger gestures*)

LARRY Security measures in response to terrorist agitation.

AMBASSADOR Right. Let's let Fishbein field this one. (*to LARRY*) Take the wheel, son?

LARRY (*Spit take*) Uhh—duhh—

> *AMBASSADOR salutes.*

LARRY President...?

> *AMBASSADOR puts hand on heart.*

LARRY (*cont.*) ...of the United States of America...

> *Pause, all expectantly look at him.*

LARRY (*cont.*) ...is not a secretary?

AMBASSDOR Exactly right, Fishbein. There won't be any complaints lodged or protests registered. (*Beat*) Now listen closely, because I'll only say this once. (*Dead serious*) If the USA has a problem with any government anywhere, the world will know. I trust that's clear.

> *Someone whistles. RENATE involuntarily stands at attention, clicks her heels.*

RENATE (*snaps*) Jawohl, Herr Botschafter!

AMBASSADOR At ease, Miss.

> *RENATE sits, bewildered.*

AMBASSADOR (*cont.*) (*Chipper, crossing out a line in his notebook*) Well: any outstanding issues? Ah yes—Fishbein, "permanently deranged." About the hashish: that's a felony, son. Fire-able. Jail-able. Now the vitally important thing is to get it out of your system before the next random, unannounced drug test, which is a week from Thursday. Pour one cup of white vinegar into a gallon of distilled water and drink it all over the course of two hours.

LARRY (*Takes a note*) Vinegar, water, two hours, sir.

AMBASSADOR That ought to do it. Oh, that and Mamamouchi. Right, miss?

LARRY blanches.

SIX Yes, sir! One Mamamouchi for J. Lawrence Fishbein coming right up!

LARRY Mama-moo--what, sir?

AMBASSADOR It's a theatre thing. For insanity. Culturally adapted. (*to SIX*) My, uh, secretary read the coverage you fine folks sent in. Great stuff. It's in the file, Fishbein. Did you even look through that thing?

LARRY Oh, boy.

AMBASSADOR Are we ready?

SIX (*And PLAYERS who are off*) Yes, sir!

AMBASSADOR Fine. I'll take my seat.

DEPUTY MINISTER is illuminated entering the house from the rear, hiccoughing, carrying a Champagne bottle and two glasses.

LARRY & RENATE (*They jump*) Serene Munificence!

DEPUTY MINISTER (*Notices AMBASSADOR*) Ah, Ambassador, an honor.

AMBASSADOR Deputy Minister.

AMBASSADOR walks down into the house, shakes hands with DEPUTY MINISTER.

DEPUTY MINISTER (*Notices LARRY*) Mr. Fishbein. Three times in one day. This festival has taken on more importance for my government. It is a key opportunity to show that we stand with our western friends against (*hiccough*) international terrorist aggression. (*Sits. Pops champagne bottle.*) Champagne, Ambassador?

AMBASSADOR Thank you.

RENATE I believe I need to go behind stage.

AMBASSADOR & DEPUTY MINISTER sit down in the audience.

AMBASSADOR Of course, miss.

RENATE Em--Larry…Toi toi toi!

RENATE exits into the wing.

LARRY (*from the stage, over footlights.*) Sir—sir—sir—

Major light change. SIGN shines bright. RENATE/THREE appears

> *onstage in costume. LARRY shrieks. Music: bullfight. THREE sits LARRY down again on his tiny chair and walks off again. SIX strides out to center, holding the storied scepter of satire, and wearing the cloak of jollity.*

SIX Distinguished guests, Excellency, Serene Munificence, rulers and subjects of this Central Asian so-called republic, The West Laughs! Comic Theatre Festival. Performers, esteemed audience: prepare for— the Investiture of the Mamamouchi!

> *PLAYERS don Inquisition-type robes. LARRY is prodded, and poked, with sticks and swords and instruments, notably the scepter. He runs away from the impulses, comments, rods, and people. A cape is brushed over his face occasionally: he has become a Toro. This cape is, of course, the famous cloak of jollity. A little curtain is fitted over his head during one pass.*

PLAYERS Toro! Olé! Toro!

LARRY Excuse me? I'm in the dark. Sorry, I can't see. Excuse me. Pardon me.

> *Bull horns are put on him. When his head emerges from the cape each time, his personal curtain is lifted and he's hit by the scepter. Instead of "Olé" people cry:*

ALL Oy vey!

> *The cape is lifted one last time, and LARRY is sitting in the seat of honor, the emperor's box, laurel, etc. surrounded by hooded torturers.*

TORTURER 1 (TWO) Does comedy serve the state?

LARRY Um—

ALL WRONG!

> *They beat him.*

TORTURER 2 (FOUR) Which is more radical, sex or laughter?

LARRY I'm sorry, I really don't—

ALL Wrong!

> *They beat him. He squirms to avoid the stick.*

TORTURER 1 (TWO) What is the difference between a role and a character?

LARRY J. Lawrence Fishbein, US Embassy!

ALL WRONG!

They beat him.

SIX (*across the footlights*) Care to try one, Imperial Highnesses?

AMBASSADOR Sure. A train leaves Skokie for Naperville at 9:10 a.m., accelerating at a rate of 0.6 meters per second squared. How long before it reaches 60 mph?

LARRY is silent.

SIX Beat him!

They beat him.

LARRY Please, stop! What have I done?

AMBASSADOR Penalty question: at a top speed of 62 mph, what time does the train reach Joliet?

LARRY (*miserable*) Can I have a pen and paper?

ALL WRONG!

They beat him.

SIX Your Serene Munificence?

AMBASSADOR Deputy Minister, do you have a question for him?

DEPUTY MINISTER Oh no, my curiosity is satisfied. (*to AMBASSADOR*) More champagne? (*Pours.*)

SIX Our theatre is interactive.

DEPUTY MINISTER Very well. What is the approximate population density of this country?

LARRY (*Pause, harrowed*) Around sixty?

DEPUTY MINISTER Per square mile or kilometer?

LARRY —Kilometer?

DEPUTY MINISTER (*To AMBASSADOR.*) Fairly close. Although by tomorrow it will be closer to fifty.

AMBASSADOR & ALL WRONG!

They all beat him. LARRY plays dead.

SIX Now we're getting somewhere!

ALL Oy vey!

A Yiddish song, "Oy Vey Tate," from A Khasene in Shtetl, *strikes up, PLAYERS singing.*

SIX Commence the investiture. Bring forth the aspirant to Mamamouchi.

FOUR He's right here.

> *The comedians jubilantly beat one another.*

DEPUTY MINISTER What language is that? Is it—Swiss German?

AMBASSADOR No, it's Yid…(*Warily, drawn out*) Yeeeees. Swiss German.

> *They beat LARRY with the stick, jubilate. Continued Yiddish singing.*

AMBASSADOR (*cont.*) Come on, Deputy Minister, give him a whack or two. It's part of the performance.

DEPUTY MINISTER In the interest of cultural understanding.

> *DEPUTY MINISTER walks up to the stage and whacks him with the proffered scepter. LARRY howls. Singing continues, now in a sole, plaintive female voice.*

LARRY (*Woozy*) Great Aunt Rose? (*Silence*) Tante Rose?

SIX What? (*Silence*)

SIX (*Mock fury*) Whaaaat?—You. Are. Exactly Right!

GREAT AUNT ROSE (*FOUR in a shawl, with a Yiddish accent, appears on her walker*) Hello, Lawrence!

LARRY But Great Aunt Rose—you're dead.

GREAT AUNT ROSE Bubbeleh, you don't look so good yourself.

LARRY Great Aunt Rose—

GREAT AUNT ROSE You're not eating enough. You should really take…the scepter of satire! (*Bonks him on the head with it*) Proceed with the Mamamouchi!

ALL Mamamouchi!

> *LARRY starts muttering.*

GREAT AUNT ROSE Mamamouchi.

ALL Mamamouchi!

> *Singing continues. Actor begins to ready a horrible implement while LARRY is bound. The implement is a tickle machine, which begins to be employed. Music out.*

SIX Do you think this is funny? (*Pause*) Do you think this is funny?

LARRY Yes?

TWO The kid's got class.

ALL Mamamouchi! Mamamouchi!

> *SIX ceremonially displays the shining, very goofy garment and holds it to the light. Very, very seriously:*

SIX I bestow upon you the cloak of jollity.

> *They put the cloak on him. Pause. Tableau vivant.*

FOUR And the scepter.

SIX And the scepter of satire.

> *SIX ceremonially displays the scepter and anoints LARRY with it.*

LARRY Mamamouchi?

SIX The Mamamouchi is invested.

> *All pose expectantly waiting for applause. Curtain closes.*

Act III Scene III

*The Great Gathering Place of the People
All present.
AMBASSADOR and DEPUTY MINISTER applaud politely.
Curtain opens.*

DEPUTY MINISTER Very good. (*Claps his hands twice.*) Bring in the audience! (*To AMBASSADOR*) More champagne?

AMBASSADOR Ah—I believe the audience is coming tomorrow night, Deputy Minister.

DEPUTY MINISTER Oh, it's all the same.

AMBASSADOR (*To SIX*) Is there more, ma'am?

SIX Excellencies, Serene Munificences: we offer up a dainty morsel to your palates: an exotic tale of loyalty, justice, and brutally authoritarian statecraft. An amusing tidbit of a tale, fraught with adventure and heroism, basted in delicious humor, our scene laid in a far-off land in a far-off time—

TWO Enough already!

SIX Worthies, I give you *The Completely Justified Security Measures Against Terrorist Agitation*!

DEPUTY MINISTER Good title!

Stagehands move around the set.

AMBASSADOR (*whispers up to Larry onstage*) What the hell is this, Fishbein?

LARRY (*getting made up*) It's in the file, sir. (*Rising intonation*)

AMBASSADOR Well, Deputy Minister, this all seems to be in order— shall we?

DEPUTY MINISTER Thank you, Ambassador. I will stay for this one. I am intrigued.

THREE Do you know your part, Larry?

LARRY No.

TWO Oh, boy. Well, neither does Medusa over here.

FOUR Well, I never! (*To LARRY*) Improvise, love.

THREE (*To LARRY*) Here's the situation, Larry…(*whispers to him*)

SIX The West Laughs!

The Completely Justified Security Measures Against Terrorist Agitation

Light change. A length of pipe around shoulder-height traverses the stage. A little shack SL. TWO walks along the pipeline, whistling. In a jovial, artificial voice:

TWO My, but this pipeline carrying vital resources is long! I, a government deputy, walk along it to ensure that the President has uninterrupted access to this lucrative resource.

AMBASSADOR (*hurried, to DEPUTY MINISTER*) You know, Deputy Minister, I have an incredible single malt collection, would you care to—

DEPUTY MINISTER Shh—I'm watching the show. I love lucrative resources!

TWO Oho! I see a little house. In it lives the man who operates this pipeline. I'd like to have a word with him, on the President's business.

LARRY, as MAN, in the little shack. Strokes his beard with one hand, and with the other strokes the head of his daughter, THREE, who crouches at his feet in a headscarf. TWO "knocks" three times. THREE goes to "door," opens it subserviently, crouches back down at LARRY's feet.

LARRY (*looks around, uncertain in the lights*) H-hello.

TWO Hello, my good man! I am a government deputy, come on business of the President.

THREE Prezidenti eng donolikdir.

LARRY H-hello. (*TWO and THREE look at him.*) Can I—offer you some tea? My wife (*they shake their heads no*)—girlfriend (*shake heads no*)—lover (*shake heads no*)—mother (*shake heads no*)—daughter will fetch some.

THREE looks around, mousy and stricken, runs off with a little squeal.

TWO Thank you, but I do not think there will be time for tea. You see, I am here to liquidate you.

LARRY What?

TWO The President—

LARRY —he is most wise.

TWO —Quite so. The President needs access to these resources.

LARRY He has access to these resources!

TWO He needs direct access to these resources.

LARRY I built the pipeline, and all I keep is a pittance for maintaining it!

TWO Then rejoice, because I am relieving you of that responsibility.

LARRY I bring foreign investment. I pay extra taxes. I volunteer with the Army.

TWO All that is administerable.

LARRY I commissioned that gigantic bronze rotating statue of the President.

TWO It is a lovely piece. Just the same—

LARRY Only a tyrant would rob me of my personal property, not a great leader like our President!

TWO Did you call our President a tyrant?

LARRY No!

> *TWO ventriloquizes a distant yell, "Tyrant!"*

LARRY Where did that come from? Who said that?

TWO So you are a terrorist agitator. How unfortunate for you.

> *Siren wailing, TWO cuffs LARRY, transports him to jail, behind bars which LARRY holds up, at the courthouse.*

LARRY No, I'm not!

> *Another cry of "Tyrant." TWO paces and smokes in front of imprisoned LARRY.*

TWO An unrepentant terrorist agitator. And you've infected your family with your anti-social poison.

> *THREE as daughter is led out, also holding bars. She wails. Is led off.*

TWO And your business partners.

> *FOUR and SIX appear with bars. Wail. Exit. More shouts of "tyrant."*

TWO The situation is getting out of hand. Do you see what you've done?

LARRY I'm a business man! A good citizen!

TWO Tell it to the judge. Here's another friend of yours. (*SIX as ISLAMIC CLERIC is thrown in*) So you're an Islamic fundamentalist terrorist.

LARRY No, I'm not!

TWO Yes you are, we've arrested this Islamic fundamentalist cleric.

LARRY I've never seen this man in my life!

TWO Playing tough, eh? (*Prepares a torture instrument*) Think you're a martyr for the Prophet?

LARRY No!

TWO (*aghast*) You turn your back on religion and the President? What kind of terrorist agitator are you?

LARRY No kind!

TWO The most dangerous kind!

> THREE, FOUR, SIX *gather in front of the house under a sign that reads "Tyrant."*

THREE, FOUR, SIX Tyrant!

TWO You see what you've done, you animal?

LARRY I'm a loyal businessman!

TWO Transport him to the ministry.

> *Under a siren,* LARRY *is transported. Once in his new cell, masked men torture and electrocute him.* LARRY *shrieks, "Ah!" "Ooh!" "Aah, it hurts!" He is transported back to the courthouse. The "crowd" reassembles in front of the courthouse.* LARRY *is pushed through into the courtroom. The Judge,* SIX, *is on the platform SL, in robe and wig. Pounds the gavel.* LARRY *is led, shackled, up to the other platform and stands in a cage.*

FOUR (*from crowd*) Tyrant!

SIX Order in the court.

THREE Tyrant!

SIX Remove that person. Order in the court.

THREE & FOUR Tyrant!

SIX Very well. Clear the court.

> TWO *lobs a grenade. Explosion. Running and screaming.*

SIX Where were we? Ah yes. Your family and business associates are currently in parallel trials. You are charged with treason, Islamic terrorism, and atheism.

LARRY I plead—

SIX We have witnessed your terrorist agitation in this very court. Your guilt is not in question.

LARRY When will we be sentenced?

SIX After the punishment. The investigation is ongoing.

LARRY But I thought my guilt was not in question.

SIX Good point. Lead out the prisoner.

LARRY (*As he is led out*) Wait! Wait! I'm a businessman!

> THREE and FOUR chant "Down With the Tyrant!"

TWO (*in trenchcoat and sunglasses, on loudspeaker, planting a bomb*) Clear the courthouse square immediately. Oh no—look over there!

> *Explosion.*

TWO (*on loudspeaker*) Some terrorist planted a bomb! Oh no—look over there! (*plants another bomb*) Another bomb! The courthouse is burning. Strict security measures are in effect. Remain calm.

> *TWO grabs LARRY and whisks him off to the Ministry building, casually shooting into the crowd.*

TWO (*loudspeaker*) Return to your homes. (*TWO ties up LARRY, tests an electrode. Lights dim and buzz.*) The chief terrorist agitators have been killed. By the, uh, other terrorist agitators. Yeah, that's it. The rival terrorist agitators.

> *TWO trades trench coat for a bloody lab coat.*

LARRY No!—no!

TWO (*loudspeaker*) Additional security measures remain in force. Foreign journalists are instructed to leave the country immediately.

> *TWO slaps LARRY, hits him with the electrode. Buzz, lights dim.*

TWO (*loudspeaker*) Television and radio signals have been suspended until further notice.

> *THREE as DAUGHTER is brought on, tied up, slapped, hit with electrode.*

TWO (*loudspeaker*) And don't forget not to tune in tomorrow at 8 o'clock for an international, intercultural exchange. The West Laughs! Comic Performance Festival not-broadcast not-live from the Great Gathering Place of the People.

> *Enter SIX as GOON, carrying a palette of knives and torture implementa. SIX sharpens two ghoulish knives against each other.*

A cry of "Down with the tyrant!" A single volley of fire. Lights focus on TWO, SIX, and an unconscious LARRY. TWO picks up one of the torture instruments, tests the blade with his thumb, pricks himself.

TWO Ow! (*sucks his finger. Lights focus on him, then out.*)

LARRY, TWO, THREE, FOUR, range on either side of SIX, who throws off her goon coat.

SIX Ladies and gentlemen, The West Laughs! (*They stand, expecting applause.*)

AMBASSADOR, flushed, whispers angrily up to LARRY.

AMBASSDOR Fishbein, I'll have your head for this. (*To DEPUTY MINISTER*) Deputy Minister, I offer a full official apology and my personal regrets for this—outrage…

AMBASSADOR sees that DEPUTY MINISTER is on his feet, applauding slowly and passionately.

DEPUTY MINISTER But Ambassador, that was…charming! (*Raises his glass to the performers*) Bravo! Bravo!

AMBASSADOR There's no—problem?

DEPUTY MINISTER Never again will I claim that the art of the West is tired and irrelevant.

SIX Thank you, Imperial Excellencies and Munificences. Allow us to present for you the next piece in The West Laughs! Comic Theatre Festival.

LARRY Performers!

SIX Excuse me?

LARRY Prepare for—<u>The Piss</u>!

AMBASSADOR Fishbein?

LARRY Mamamouchi!

DEPUTY MINISTER No need to perform any more for us. We shall see it all tomorrow. Besides, I believe I read this one.

AMBASSADOR How did you like it, Deputy Minister?

DEPUTY MINISTER There's a lot to think about.

SIX We thank you humbly for your patient audience, worthy Excellencies and Munificences, and…

DEPUTY MINISTER empties his bottle and gets up.

DEPUTY MINISTER All right.

AMBASSADOR Deputy Minister, I suppose I'll see you again tomorrow night?

DEPUTY MINISTER I suppose so.

LARRY (*wide-eyed*) Our art and our happiness are incomplete without your presence, Munificence.

AMBASSADOR (*wary*) Riiight. Very well. Deputy Minister, I have an appointment and have to say goodbye.

DEPUTY MINISTER As do I. Shall we leave together?

AMBASSADOR With pleasure.

SIX Worthies, we have another scene for your delectation, would you—

AMBASSADOR Go on without us. We'll see you tomorrow—at the reception. Good night.

> *PLAYERS are confused.*

DEPUTY MINISTER Good night. Your man's done good work, Ambassador.

AMBASSADOR (*Pause*) Good work, Fishbein.

LARRY Oh, all in a day's work, Excellency! (*Bows*)

AMBASSADOR I'm—recommending you for a promotion. Now please—

LARRY (*from stage*) Oh, grand! That's really—super, sir.

AMBASSADOR Now please: get some rest, son.

LARRY Oh, I'll stay on a little longer—we have to confirm the precise modalities for tomorrow night. You know: the reception! But thank you, Ambassador. (*sweetly waving*) Good night!

> *During the following, AMBASSODOR and DEPUTY MINISTER move towards exit slowly, arm in arm. As they leave, LARRY begins to hum "The Star-Spangled Banner," louder and louder, singing the lyrics and mouth-trumpeting in snatches.*

AMBASSADOR Deputy Minister, it's not official yet, but I'll be making a statement tomorrow, about Mandijan.

DEPUTY MINISTER The world looks to America for truth and light.

AMBASSADOR The gist of it is this: we believe that security measures may have engendered isolated incidents of disproportionate force. But the entire situation all stemmed from illegal demonstrations, and we trust the local judiciary to investigate more fully.

DEPUTY MINISTER I understand your position.

LARRY (*Singing*) "What so proudly we hailed"

DEPUTY MINISTER You know, Ambassador, the President will attend the performance tomorrow night.

AMBASSADOR Deputy Minister, what a signal honor that is. How wonderful to ratify the friendship between our sister republics (*gesture*) in these violent times.

> *They walk up a platform upstage, turn towards each other, and embrace in a Brezhnev/Honecker-style kiss. They hold. A long moment. PLAYERS look at LARRY.*

FOUR How do you feel, Larry?

LARRY "O'er the laaaaaaaand of the free…" I'm—oh no, I feel—I'm worried—quick, get me some makeup. (*SIX hits him with the pouf.*) I'm going crazy!

TWO He's a lunatic.

FOUR He's a lunatic!

> *LARRY jumps up, starts whooping and running around the stage, à la Curly Fine.*

LARRY I'm a lunatic! (*Slaps SIX*) I'm a lunatic! (*Slaps TWO*) Oh no, I'm out of control! I'm a lunatic!

> *LARRY gooses THREE. LARRY runs after her. Twits AMBASSADOR and DEPUTY MINISTER à la Looney Tunes. They look out a moment, go back to kissing. LARRY tears away after THREE.*

LARRY Mamamouchi!

TWO (*runs around*) Wait—I'm a lunatic, too!

SIX What the hell is Larry doing?

TWO I'm a lunatic! (*TWO slaps SIX.*)

FOUR No, you're not. (*Slaps him. SIX slaps him.*)

TWO (*Slaps SIX*) Yes, I am!

FOUR & SIX (*Slap TWO*) No, you're not!

> *THREE is pushed back onstage, followed by a volley of flowers thrown from off. THREE straightens her clothes, walks towards the*

others looking sad and puzzled. PLAYERS put on masks. LARRY emerges, looking haggard, carrying flowers. All look at LARRY. FOUR removes mask, walks slowly towards LARRY.

CATHERINE Well, Larry, what's it going to be?

LARRY (*Uncertainly*) Ladies—

PIERRE-FRANÇOIS (*Removing mask*) Alors, Larry? I am sorry, but we cannot—

LARRY Ladies and gentlemen—

AMBASSADOR (*Looking briefly away from his kiss*) Fishbein?

LARRY Mamamouchi, sir. (*muttering*) Mamamouchi. Mamamouchi.

AMBASSADOR shrugs, returns to his embrace with DEPUTY MINISTER.

RENATE (*Removes mask. Great regret.*) Ach nein, Schatzi (*takes LARRY's arm*). You are mad.

CATHERINE And you're surprised, love?

LARRY (*Shaking now*) Ladies and gentlemen—

SIGN shines bright. Blinks in and out. PLAYERS all assemble around LARRY. Masks on.

EMBASSY SECRETARY (*Removing mask*) Come on already, Lar! What does the West do? (*Slaps LARRY, replaces mask.*)

LARRY (*Crazy, with decision*) Mama-goddamn-mouchi! Ladies and gentlemen—give me a goddamn mask! (*SIX hands him a mask*) Ladies and gentlemen—the West (*Bullhorn, gunshots, a loud explosion. Confetti falls*) Laughs!

Lights out. Sign blinks out. Curtain.

END OF PLAY

About the Author

Martin Schwartz is a playwright, director, and cultural advocate. His original works *Cockroach, Comedy Ballet, TUTOR,* and *StormStressLenz* have been performed by Dark Porch Theatre, of which he is co-artistic director, in San Francisco and Phoenix, winning awards including Best of San Francisco Fringe (2009, 2013) and the *Phoenix New Times'* 10 Best (2012).

A graduate of University of California, San Diego, and the University of Chicago and a longtime cultural affairs specialist with the Swiss Department of Foreign Affairs, he lives with his wife in San Francisco.

MORE PLAYS FROM EXIT PRESS

Woyzeck, Pelleas and Melisande, Ubu Roi: translated by Rob Melrose

"Rob Melrose is a kind of magician, and his theater, Cutting Ball, is one of the most exciting and integrity-filled enterprises going in the sometimes-shabby field of the American theater. These translations, lucid and sharp, are a beautiful testimony to the value of Rob's achievement." — Oskar Eustis

Three Plays by Mark Jackson

"Playwright/director Mark Jackson has made his name as a first-class theatrical provocateur. Gutsy showmanship, brainy literary instincts and laser-sharp satire mark his canon." — San Jose Mercury News This collection of plays by Mark Jackson includes three plays based on incredible historic events: *God's Plot, Mary Stuart,* and *Salomania.*

Songs of Hestia: Plays From the 2010 San Francisco Olympians Festival

Playwrights Nirmala Nataraj, Bennett Fisher, Stuart Eugene Bousel, Claire Rice, and Evelyn Jean Pine adapt some of Western culture's oldest stories, illuminating our present-day concerns with imagination, creativity, curiosity and passion.

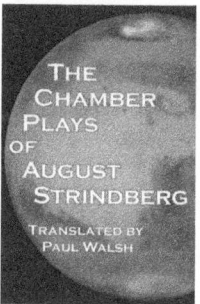

The Chamber Plays of August Strindberg translated by Paul Walsh

The Ghost Sonata, The Pelican, The Black Glove, Storm, and *Burned House.* Yale professor Paul Walsh provides modern translations while keeping Strindberg's "curiosity and his strangeness as specific and opaque as they are in the Swedish."

EXIT Press is the publishing division of EXIT Theatre, a San Francisco theater company founded in 1983. EXIT Press is distributed by Small Press Distribution of Berkeley, California. www.exitpress.org

www.ingramcontent.com/pod-product-compliance
Lightning Source LLC
Chambersburg PA
CBHW020015050426
42450CB00005B/476